BOOK ONE
THE ART OF DEFENDING
Phase Play and 11v11 Defending

CHAPTER FOUR

The Art of Defending
Part Two

Phase Play and 11v11

Wayne Harrison

REEDSWAIN

**Library of Congress
Cataloging - in - Publication Data**

by Wayne Harrison
    The Art of Defending
      Part Two - Phase Play and 11v11

ISBN No. 1-59164-033-4
Lib. of Congress Catalog No. 2002094148
© 2002

Editing
Bryan R. Beaver

Printed by
DATA REPRODUCTIONS
Auburn, Michigan

Reedswain Publishing
612 Pughtown Road
Spring City, PA 19475
800.331.5191
www.reedswain.com
info@reedswain.com

CHAPTER ONE

INTRODUCTION TO DEFENDING

Following on from the first book on defending which covers 1 v 1 through to 8 v 8 defending, the final progression is to working on defending in an 11 v 11 game situation. That is what this book is all about.

To begin we will be looking at defending through the thirds of the field, breaking it down to show how the various units defend.

We will be building the defending theme as in the previous book around the key points in defending, which are pressure, support, cover / balance, recovery, tracking, double teaming, regaining possession and compactness.

The defending team is represented by numbered players only. The lettered team is always the attacking team.

Defending principles can be categorized into a logical process for the coach to follow and implement in training. They can be broken down into the following key coaching points:

1. PRESSURE
2. SUPPORT
3. COVER / BALANCE
4. RECOVER
5. TRACK
6. DOUBLE TEAM
7. REGAINS & COMPACTNESS / ADVANCE

What does this all mean?

PRESSURE

This is when the individual defender closes down a player on the ball to exert pressure on him to give the ball up. It can result in the player on the ball being pressured into making a bad pass, mis-controlling it, or the defender being able to tackle the player and dispossess him by either kicking the ball away or challenging and winning possession. These instances all result in possession being lost by the attacking team due to the pressure exerted by the first defender.

Pressure does not always result in a change of possession immediately, so the defender can jockey the attacker to stop his forward momentum and give time to teammates to get into position to help win the ball back.

SUPPORT

This is the position taken up by the second defender to act as help for the first defender. The first defender, by his stance, can show / force the attacker towards the support player (second defender).We will talk later about angles and distances of support and communication with the pressuring player. These are the three essentials that are needed for the support player to be effective.

COVER / BALANCE

This refers to the positions of the next line of players away from the first two defenders, particularly the third defender who is next closest to the pressure and support players. This player provides a balance (1st, 2nd, and 3rd defender) behind the pressure and support players. Beyond this third defender you can work with the next closest players and integrate their positioning into your coaching session.

RECOVER

Players in position on the field in front of where the ball is being defended must make it a priority to run back and position behind the ball, if possible between their own goal and the ball that is in the attacking team's possession. They recover back (recovery runs) to help the team by getting more people between the ball and their own goal to make it more difficult for the attacking team to score. They must recover back along the shortest route so they get back as quickly as possible but into a position where they are most effective in terms of the positions of the ball and the opponents.

TRACK

The attacking team's players will make forward runs into dangerous positions on the field and this is where defending players need to follow or track their runs to mark them and prevent them from getting free and able to affect the game. Tracking runs can be short or long depending on the distance of the opponent's runs.

DOUBLE TEAM

It is possible to help the pressing player win back possession of the ball by closing down the space (pressuring) around the attacking player on the ball from another angle, preferably from the other side to where the first pressuring player is positioned. This is almost closing the player on the ball down from his blind side and can be very effective in regaining possession of the ball due to the fact that the attacker doesn't see the second defender coming so can't take immediate action to avoid having the ball taken off his. In some circumstances triple teaming can occur where three players all close the player on the ball down simultaneously and this can prove very effective in regaining possession of the ball.

REGAINING POSSESSION AND COMPACTNESS

Here the defending team has won back the ball and are now the attacking team and look to play it forward as soon as possible. As the play is developed up the field it is important the team push up the field to add continued support to the player on the ball, but also to affect the positions of the opponents and take them away from their goal should possession be lost again. The whole team moves forward and this will result in the compactness of the players from the back to the front of the team.

COACHING METHODOLOGY

To be effective a coach should be able to change to different coaching methods to suit the moment. We all have our own style; some do it quietly, some are more demonstrative, and some are more vocal (but don't commentate). As long as it is done in a positive manner and creates positive results, all styles can be effective.

Coaching Style is based on personality, temperament, our philosophies on how the game should be played and on the ages and abilities of the players we are working with. There is no one universal style, every coach is different.

Coaching Method is different, the methods you use to coach are important in getting the best out of your players and you should be able to base your coaching around three different methods which can be implemented in various degrees at different times.

COMMAND, QUESTION AND ANSWER AND GUIDED DISCOVERY

1. COMMAND METHOD

The coach decides, the players listen and comply but do they really listen, do they learn or most importantly DO THEY UNDERSTAND?

Using this method the coach can't be sure if the players understand what they are doing or why they are doing it, or if they are simply following directions.

Were you right in what you told them?

For example you tell a player to move to a certain position on the field and he does it. Does he know why he needs to be there? Maybe, but you cannot be certain. In a game situation will he know where to go?

2. QUESTION AND ANSWER METHOD

The coach tries to stimulate the player into a response to a direct singular question. For example, "Where should you pass the ball in that situation?". The player needs to think for himself and you know immediately if he understands or not by his response.

3. GUIDED DISCOVERY METHOD

The coach leads the players to make their own decisions. For example: "Show me where you should go to help the player on the ball". Again the players have to think for themselves and are more likely to remember and learn from their self determined action.

Soccer is a game of the moment and players, not coaches need to decide at that moment what they should do on the field and we need to help them to make that decision for themselves. What we have is a Command Method (autocratic / bossy) and a Co-Operative Method (democratic / guiding) but sometimes also a good coaching approach may involve saying nothing, letting them play / practice with no direction. Just watch them. This is more important than some realize.

WHY CO-OPERATIVE?

1.   It helps players become thinkers and make their own decisions.
2.   Fosters relations between coach and player by sharing the decision making process.
3.   Players enjoy it more.
4.   As well as having skills, players develop the ability to change situations, exhibit discipline and maintain concentration.

HOW DOES IT HELP THE COACH?

The coach needs more skill and knowledge. Because players can have several solutions to one problem, they are seldom absolutely right or wrong, but you as the coach need to have an answer. This improves you as a coach as you yourself need to think more deeply about your solutions to problems. External factors can influence the method used. For example, a large group of unfamiliar players need more of the Command Method where a smaller familiar group of players need more of a Co-Operative Method of coaching.

CONCLUSION

Based on the above discussion it is clear that soccer is a game of free flowing play and the players need to be developed to be the decision makers much of the time. The coach needs to help them get there by encouraging them in training to work it out for themselves and, when they can't, guide them to the right decision. Game situations are difficult because you often don't have time to ask "where should you be now?" but over a period of time and with patience the players will take on more responsibility on and off the field and improve their performance because of it. A by- product of this which must not be overlooked is that the coach himself will improve his ability and knowledge as a consequence of using this approach.

HOW TO ORGANIZE A SESSION PLAN

1. ORGANIZE THE EQUIPMENT (BIBS, BALLS AND CONES)
2. COACH ONLY ONE TEAM AT A TIME TO AVOID CONFUSION
3. COACH (AFFECT THE ATTITUDE OF) EACH INDIVIDUAL PLAYER IN THAT TEAM
4. STAY ON THE SAME THEME
5. USE DESIGNATED START POSITIONS TO BEGIN EACH PRACTICE TO PAINT THE PICTURE YOU WANT TO CREATE
6. LIST THE KEY COACHING POINTS
7. THINK INDIVIDUAL / UNIT / TEAM – SIMPLE TO COMPLEX AND DEVELOP LOGICAL PROGRESSIONS INTO THE SESSION
8. SPECIFY THE SIZE OF AREA USED AND MAKE IT RELEVANT TO THE NUMBERS AND ABILITY OF PLAYERS USED
9. DIVIDE THE FIELD INTO THIRDS FOR EASIER POINTS OF REFERENCE IN SMALL - SIDED GAMES
10. USE TARGET GOALS, TARGET PLAYERS, OR LINES FOR OPPONENTS TO PLAY TO IN PHASE PLAYS AND FUNCTIONS
11. ISOLATE THE AREAS AND PLAYERS IN FUNCTIONAL PRACTICES TO KEEP IT SPECIFIC
12. USE OFFSIDE WHERE NECESSARY FOR REALISM
13. COACHING METHOD: FREEZE THE COACHING MOMENT (STOP, STAND STILL), REVIEW WHAT WENT WRONG, RE-RUN SLOWLY (CAN BE WALKING PACE), RE-CREATE THE SET UP AND GO AT MATCH SPEED. LET THEM PLAY
14. USE A QUESTIONING / GUIDING COACHING METHOD RATHER THAN COMMAND
15. FOR ATTACKING THEMES LIMIT THE NUMBER OF TOUCHES THE OPPONENTS HAVE IF THEY WIN THE BALL

16. FOR DEFENDING THEMES LIMIT THE NUMBER OF TOUCHES THE DEFENDING TEAM HAS WHEN THEY WIN THE BALL.THIS ENSURES THE OPPONENTS HAVE THE BALL FOR THE DEFENDERS TO TRY TO WIN BACK

BASIC 11 v 11 SYSTEM TO WORK FROM

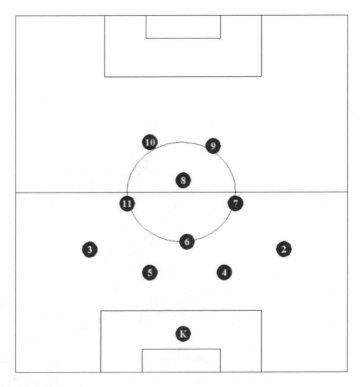

Diagram 1

For the 11 v 11 games we will be using this basic system of play most of the time to demonstrate how to defend as a team.

CHAPTER TWO

PHASE PLAY PRACTICES

DEFENDING THROUGH THE THIRDS

HOW TO PRESENT A PHASE PLAY

1. Only coach one team at a time.

2. Try to work with all the players on the team you are coaching, affecting each performance in a positive way.

3. Stay with one theme / topic at a time, don't jump from one to another during the session. This will only confuse the players.

4. Include key coaching points and list them with the session plan. Try to cover each point within the session itself.

5. Use specific start positions to begin the session.

6. In defending phase plays, since you are working with the defending team who protects the only goal, the team that needs to have the ball most of the time is the attacking team. Once the defenders win possession they should get the ball to a target goal quickly and in as few passes as possible. As soon as the defenders score in a target goal, the ball goes back to the attacking team and they begin a new attack. You can condition this by allowing the defending team only so many passes (maybe 5 passes) to get the ball to a target. After 5 passes, they lose the ball and a new phase play is set up.

7. Phase plays can involve numerous combinations ranging from 4 v 4 to 9 v 9; this can depend on the number of players you have to work with on any given day. Often the

best number is 7 v 7 or with an overload in favor of the team you are working with to help gain initial success in the session (maybe 7 v 5). For example, in a defending phase play have more defenders than attackers to help the session succeed initially, then go to equal numbers. When you get consistent success with this, go for an overload against to make it more difficult for the defenders (for example a 5 v 7 against).

8.   In an attacking phase play have 7 attacking players against 4 defending players and a keeper to help the session have the chance be a positive experience for the players you are coaching and the theme to be successful.

9.   Make it competitive by counting the number of goals scored by each team. The defending team, on winning the ball, can attack the goal and again you can use the 5 passes rule where they have to get a shot off within 5 passes. Initially have a shot on goal count as a point, then make it more competitive allowing a point only if they actually score. The attacking team scores by getting the ball to a target player.

10.   Coaching styles – Command, question and answer and guided discovery are the three methods of coaching to be used preferably. The third one, guided discovery, is the most used as it gets the players to think for themselves (though there are always situations where each style is required).

11.   Command is telling and / or showing the players what to do (doesn't leave a lot of room for the players to think for themselves and understand). Question and answer is just that; asking players to tell you what they think should happen. Guided discovery is asking players to show you they understand a coaching point by moving themselves to the proper position using their own decisions.

THE PHASE PLAY GAME PLAN SET UP

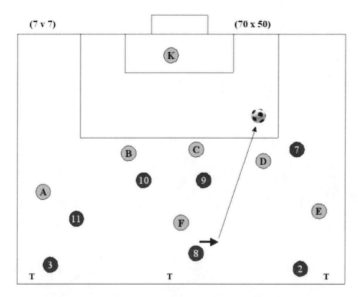

Diagram 2

1. The start position is where a player moves the ball first on their first touch to simulate open play (as opposed to a set play) and then begins the session by making the required action. This can be a pass on the second touch to another player or a pass into space or maybe a pass towards an opponent if the session is on regaining possession of the ball in the Attacking Third as above.

2. Alternatively, the coach may instigate the initial action so that the start of play is how he wants it to start.

3. The above example is a situation where the ball has to be played in behind the opponent's defensive line as it may happen in a game and the set up is such that the numbered team has to close down player (D) with the help of teammates to try to win the ball back and get a shot at goal.

4. (9) could be the player to pass the ball to begin the movement, attempting to play the ball behind (D) to get (7) in.

START POSITIONS FOR PHASE PLAYS

Coaching Points

1. Pressure
2. Support
3. Cover
4. Recover
5. Track
6. Double-Teaming
7. Compactness

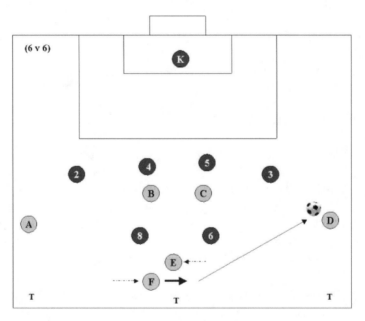

Diagram 3

1.   Start Position 1 – (E) and (F) do a crossover run and pass the ball to a teammate. This is a simple and effective start position to use to begin the practice (see above).

2.   SP 2 – You could have (A) or (D) crossing the ball into the 6 yard box for the keeper to take. The defenders are in defensive positions in the box. The keeper can then kick the ball long to (E) or (F) to control and begin the attack-

ing movement with the defenders pushing out at the same time, getting set up to defend and win the ball back.

3.   SP 3 – Have (B) or (C) shoot at goal and the keeper can kick the ball long as above.

4.   The midfield set up can be as above with a flat two in the middle or you can use the diamond midfield set up with three in midfield (or just the defensive midfielder) without the attacking midfielder at the top of the diamond. You can vary it depending on your needs for the session. This is just a simple way to set it up.

DEFENDING THROUGH THE THIRDS

DEFENDING IN THE DEFENSIVE THIRD IN A PHASE OF PLAY

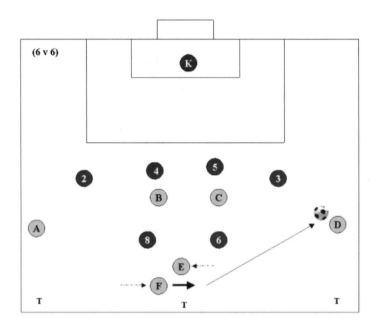

Diagram 4

1.   Begin the phase play with equal numbers to allow the defending team a chance of success from the session.

2.   Start Position – (E) and (F) do a crossover run and pass the ball to a team mate.

3.   Try to keep the ball in front of the back four and outside the penalty area.

4.   Play the offside rule to simulate true match conditions when you let it go free.

5.   Walk through it to begin and have the ball at each attacking player and show the positions of all the defenders depending on where the ball is. Explain pressure and support positions.

6.   Once the game starts, when the defenders win it they get
       the ball to the target goals, push out as a unit, reorganize
       and start again.

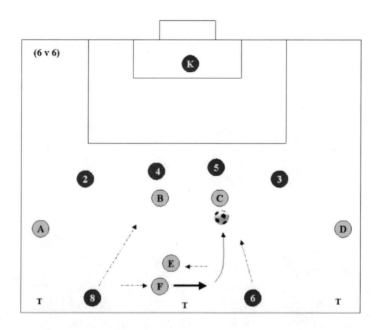

Diagram 5

1.   Increase the difficulty as the defenders get success in this
       phase play. A progression from this is have the two mid-
       fielders start in recovery positions on the wrong side of
       the ball.

2.   The coach can count to three (or more) before they can
       recover back to help the back four. This creates for a
       moment a 4 v 6 against the defending team (outfield
       players). They must try to delay the attacking team until
       the recovering midfielders get back into position to help.

3.   Recovery runs are via the shortest route back to goal in a
       straight line.

4.   Encourage the attacking team to try to break quickly to
       attack the goal to increase the difficulty for the defenders.

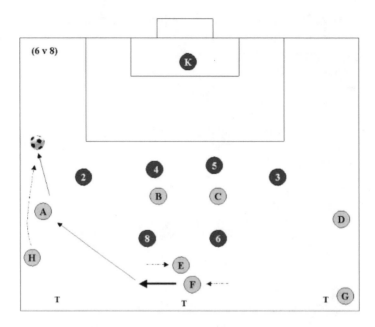

Diagram 6

1.   The next progression is introducing two wide attackers and creates a 2 v 1 in wide areas i.e. attackers get behind the defense.

2.   (A) and (H) work together to create an overlap situation in a 2 v 1 overload against (2). This may result in (H) getting into a good crossing position behind the defense. Show the adjustment of the back four and midfielders.

3.   The challenge of the defending back four is to keep the ball out of the penalty area to keep it clear for the keeper, but here the ball has gotten in behind them in a wide area so they must recover back to cover for the cross.

DEFENDING IN THE MIDDLE THIRD IN A PHASE OF PLAY

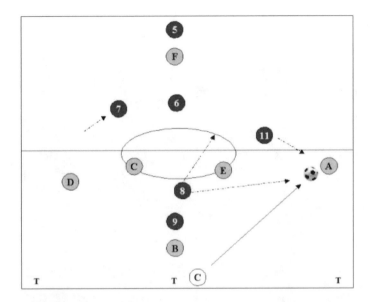

Diagram 7

1. The attacking team must run the ball over the midfield third line to score. If the defending team wins it they must pass to the target goals and play begins again. Attacking midfielders can use their one forward as a target to play off of.

2. The defensive midfield diamond works together as a unit. (8) can double up depending on where the ball is or recover back to get behind the ball and mark a player (see above). If you use a straight midfield four, then the above principle applies anyway, with (8) being the imme-diate support player for (11).

3. Looking for midfield players to:
    a) Pressure and / or win the ball.
    b) Stop the forward pass.
    c) Force play across the field.
    d) Force play back.
    e) Delay the opposition.

MIDFIELD THIRD

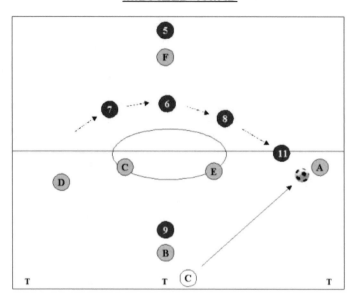

Diagram 8

Here we see that (8) has dropped into the midfield line behind the ball. An alternative position would be to double up on (A) with (11) or stay in position and keep the diamond shape. Should the ball be passed backwards, (8) may be in a good position to intercept the pass. For example, a pass from (A) to (B).

FUNCTIONS OF A DIAMOND MIDFIELD

Balance as a midfield unit

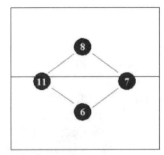

Diagram 9

Basic Diamond
shape. Players in
diagonal contact with
each other.

Keeping Defensive Shape

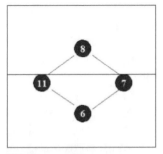

Diagram 10

A quite tight shape
close to the ball.
Spaces between players
are smaller.

Keeping Offensive Shape

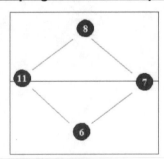

Diagram 11

Basic shape still, but
spread out to cover
more area and make
it difficult for the
opposition to mark.

Overloading Danger Area

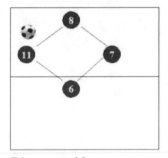

Diagram 12

Basic shape but players
get tighter to the ball and
move as a unit as the
ball moves.

I have shown also in the previous diagrams another way to use a diamond midfield in the defensive set up where (8) drops back to integrate into the other midfield three and get behind the ball. It depends how you want your team to play and/ or if you employ a double teaming philosophy for (8).

As soon as the ball is won back, (8) is encouraged to push on and take up the attacking midfield position at the top of the diamond again and the midfield shape is re-established. Switching from one to the other takes more thought and organization and often the player needs to recognize which move to make based on the situation in the game.

Alternatively, they can move around the field trying to keep their basic diamond shape both when in defensive mode and attacking mode as shown in the four diagrams above. I am attempting to show you options using this style. There is no right or wrong way, only the way that best suits your situation.

REGAINING POSSESSION IN THE ATTACKING THIRD IN A PHASE OF PLAY (7 v 7)

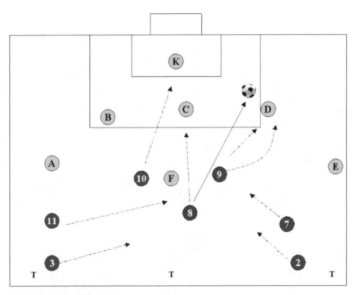

Diagram 13

If the letter team wins the ball they must play it to the target goals and play restarts. You can count the number of goals scored by the letter team (they must get the ball to a target player or score through the target goals) and the number of goals scored by the numbers team (initially they must win the ball back then get a shot on goal). Progress to a more competitive game by counting only goals that actually score.

1.   Start Position: The ball is played in behind the defender (D). How the players position on the field depends on where the pressing player shows the opponent on the ball. Here the pressing player (9) shows the player inside towards the center of the field. If we can win the ball here we have an immediate chance to shoot at goal.

2.   The other players look to fill the spaces where the ball is likely to be played and be close to an opponent to apply pressure should he receive the ball. Players must act immediately and all together when they see where the

pressing player shows the opponent on the ball. They have then the best chance to collectively win back the ball in a vital area on the field.

3.   By winning the ball back early due to players working quickly over a short distance, they can save themselves a lot of work. Allowing the opponents to clear it easily means they may get it into our defensive third and our whole team has to cover a lot more ground to recover and win back the ball in a less dangerous position for the opponents.

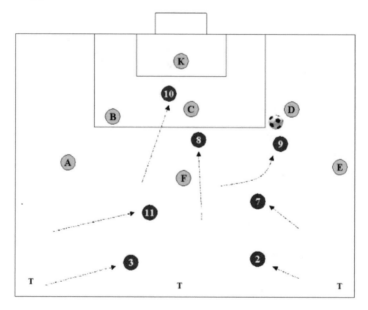

Diagram 14

1.   This diagram shows where the players should finally position themselves off the position of the pressing player. Here (D) has managed to get turned and face forward.

2.   If (D) manages to clear the ball, the pressure may force (D) to hastily clear it and make a bad pass and we have several players positioned to collect the second ball and regain possession.

3.   If the clearance is longer and the pressing player can only show (D) inside, but not win the ball or stop the forward pass, the ball is likely to be cleaned up by our center backs or defensive midfielder in an 11 v 11 game situation.

4.   Whatever happens from the three scenarios above (we win it, they kick it short under pressure, they kick it long and clear), we are at least giving ourselves a better chance to win back the ball quickly (by correct positioning) in a dangerous area where we may get a chance to shoot and perhaps score a goal.

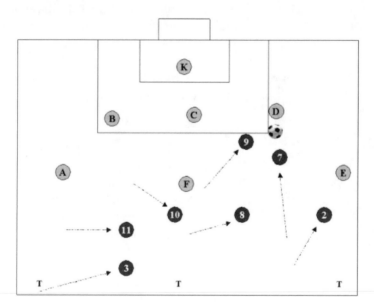

Diagram 15

1.   Pressing player (9) can't get close enough quickly enough to force the player on the ball to the inside, therefore (9) can only force (D) outside. Again the rest of the team adjusts their positions on the field off (9)'s position. This should allow them to stop the back pass for (D) to get out of trouble.

2.   If (7) is close enough he can double team (and maybe show inside) though in reality it may be that (7) will not be close enough. If (D) can play it wide to (E), then (2) will need to close off (E) quickly as the ball travels to exert the next phase of pressure on the ball.

3.   The only problem with showing outside is that if the opponents are under severe pressure they can kick the ball out of play and give themselves time to reorganize. It may be difficult to prevent this but at least we can get a set play from it and regain possession.

4.   We can change the start positions by playing a pass in behind the opponents, forcing them to try to turn and clear the ball. Try to force them inside towards their own goal. An alternate starting position is playing a ball into the box in the air and anticipating where the ball may go from the clearance should a defender win it.

ANTICIPATION AREAS AROUND THE PENALTY AREA IN A PHASE OF PLAY

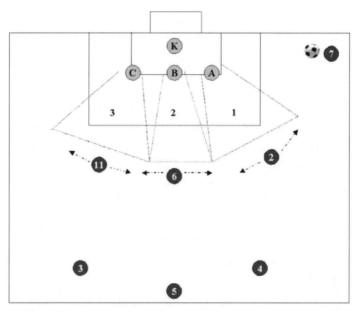

Diagram 16

1. We have regained possession of the ball and are in a position to attack the opponent's goal.

2. We haven't put the three attackers on the diagram to enable us to see where defenders may win the ball. We are working on "anticipation area" players here, not the attacking players in the box.

3. Let's assume defender (A) wins the header and "generally" will clear the ball into area (1). The same applies to the other defenders and their areas.

4. The three second line players position where they anticipate the ball will go in order to regain possession. They watch the line of flight of the ball and adjust right or left depending on where they think the ball will be cleared to e.g. the ball travels to the far post area towards defender (C), so it's likely it will be cleared into area 3. Seeing this,

(6) and (2) shuffle across quickly to help (11).

5.   It is important that if attackers can't win the first header they don't let defenders get a clean header so the ball doesn't travel very far from a clearance i.e. beyond the second line of attack.

6.   If the "anticipation area" players regain possession from the clearance, they are in a good position to keep the ball. More importantly, they get a shot at goal and we have another opportunity to score from good defending.

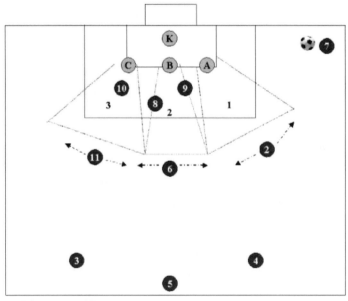

Diagram 17

1.   Here the three strikers are in the penalty box and awaiting the crossed ball.

2.   (9) attacks the near post, (8) the middle of the goal and (10) the far post area. If the defender wins the header, pressure from the attacker may affect the strength and direction of the defensive header.

3.   The ball then has a good chance of dropping into an

anticipation area for the second ball to be regained by the anticipation players around the edge of the penalty area.

4.   So while we may have lost the initial challenge with the defender winning the header, we can have a chance of winning the second challenge around the edge of the box and perhaps getting at shot or header on goal.

CHAPTER THREE

DEFENSIVE ZONING BUILDING FROM A 2 v 1 TO AN 11 v 11

MARKING ZONES AND PLAYERS AS OPPOSED TO MARKING PLAYERS

Marking zones rather than players is a good way to defend because it keeps defending players from being pulled all over the field and into bad defensive positions. Man marking often results in this because players allow themselves to be pulled out of position easily when chasing their man all over the field.

Players mark opponents who enter their zones. We want to show how marking zones prevents defending players from being pulled out of position.

ZONAL DEFENDING IN 2 v 1 AND 2 v 2 SITUATIONS

2 v 1 (25 x 15)

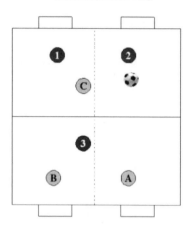

Diagram 18

1.   The set up is a 2 v 1 in each half of the field. Each defender has a goal to defend and focus on. To highlight each zone a player is responsible from a middle line to the touchline. Use cones to show the boundaries of each zone.

2.   Try two ways to work, a) each defender stays in his own quarter of the grid so he has to pass on the attacking player as he crosses over the dotted line b) or he can move between the quarters but must stay in his own half.

3.   As player (3) moves across from left to right, first (B) marks then (3) is passed on to (A) as the he moves into the other zone.

4.   Good communication skills are needed in zonal marking where players are "passed on".

5.   Develop – Players can move over the half way line.

2 v 2

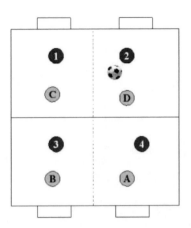

Diagram 19

1. This is a more difficult challenge with a player each to mark. Defenders must try to maintain their position and avoid crossing over each other, especially if they are two center backs.

2. This crossing over cannot always be avoided, but again good communication is essential.

3. Develop – Introduce side players to link up in support situations but stay outside the area.

SHADOW DEFENDING INTRODUCING OPPONENTS

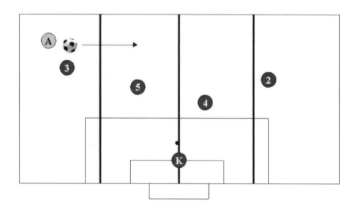

Diagram 20

1.   To establish where zones begin and end, use cones to represent boundaries (thick lines in the diagrams).

2.   (A) moves across with the ball and the players adjust as (A) enters their zone. Do it slowly to begin until they get the idea. Maintaining the shape through zonal marking ensures a well organized defensive set up and eliminates the big holes created by man marking where opponents pull defenders out of position.

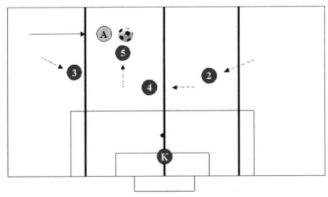

Diagram 21

1. Players close in around the ball, filling the central spaces.

2. Good communication is essential here. Each player is responsible for his own zone. This type of defending, when done correctly, is less physically demanding than a man marking style of play where players have to track their immediate opponents.

ZONAL DEFENDING WITH A BACK FOUR

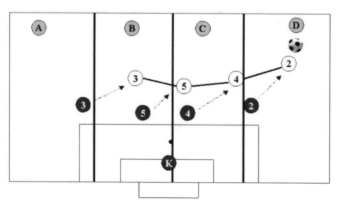

Diagram 22

1. Introduce four opponents in static positions. They pass the ball between themselves and keep it to allow the defenders to get their shape right and for the coach to adjust them if needed. At this point defenders don't try to win the ball, just shadow it wherever it goes.

2. Work the ball across the field. The second center back must try to be the deepest player, for example (5) above (always a central player if possible).

3. We want to avoid a situation where the widest defender is furthest back as this allows central attackers to move behind central defenders for a through ball. If the center back is the deepest defending player, even if the attacking opponents break through centrally, at least this defender is closer to affecting / stopping the move and preventing the opponent from scoring.

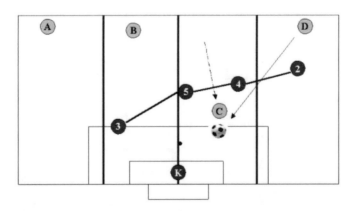

Diagram 23

1.   Here (C) makes a run in behind (4) and is played onside by (3) from a very wide position. (3) cannot affect the play because he is too far away from the ball.

2.   If (5) was the back player, he would be much closer to the danger area and more able to defend effectively against (C), even if (C) timed the run to stay on side.

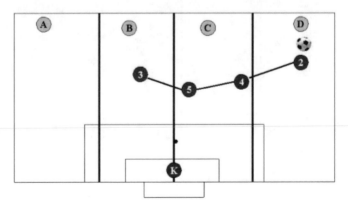

Diagram 24

ADJUSTMENT OF THE DEFENDING FOUR AS THE BALL TRAVELS

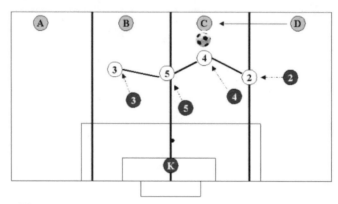

Diagram 25

The ball is passed to (C) and the defenders adjust accordingly, marking players, marking zones or a combination of both (closer to the ball mark the player, further away mark the zone) depending on where the ball is.

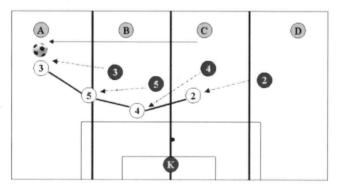

Diagram 26

This is called marking in advance of the ball. For example, (2) is marking space but can close (D) as the ball travels. The players' body stances must be open so they can see the ball and the player they are marking.

ZONAL DEFENDING AGAINST AN ATTACKING SIX

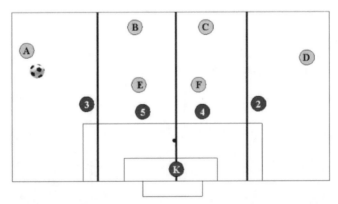

Diagram 27

Introduce two forwards to make a 4 v 6, open the play up and coach the back four accordingly. You can introduce recovering players to support the back four.

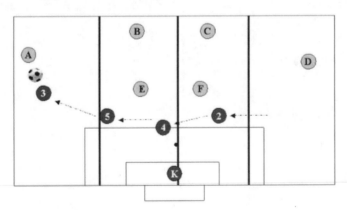

Diagram 28

Adjustment of the back four to close down the ball, players marking in advance of the ball. Moving from the left: (3) is purely marking the player, (5) is a combination of both, (4) is the same but marking spacemore, (2) is purely zone marking (compare the distances). Introduce two more wide players (4 v 8) as a progression.

ZONAL DEFENDING IN A 4 v 4

Introduce four goals for each team to defend.

Players take their shape from 4 references: the rope, the zone, the goal, and the opposing players.

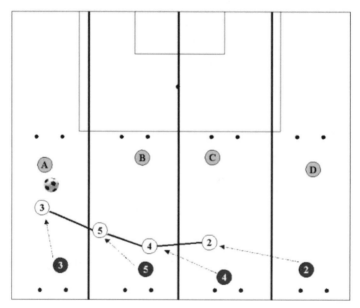

Diagram 29

1.   This begins as a 4 v 4 game working on zonal marking (marking space). Use a rope to tie the back four together so they have to move as a unit. It can be a back four or a midfield four, the responsibilities are the same. There are four 5 yard wide goals on each team to defend. Teams can score in any goal at any time. Each team must work in a unit of four (or a three with three goals to defend).Each goal is zoned off for a player to fill.

2.   To maintain a shape, players defend their own goals but must support their teammates to regain possession. By focusing on a goal of their own to defend, they are able to keep a sense of shape as a unit. They have to think about defending their goal, keeping their zone, supporting the pressing player and marking their own player.

3.   Players must try to maintain their shape and not be
        moved around by the opposition as they would if they
        were marking players. Players must squeeze centrally
        behind the ball.

ZONAL DEFENDING IN A 4 v 4

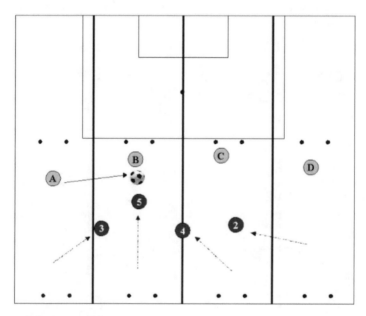

Diagram 30

1.   The ball is passed to (B) and the defenders adjust accord-
        ingly. They squeeze centrally behind the ball, marking
        space but close enough in distance to close their immedi-
        ate opponent down. For example, (2) judges position by
        where the ball is and where the immediate opponent is,
        so if the ball is passed to (D) there is time to close down
        and get to him.

2.   Show the positions of the players in relation to their own
        goals. Can the opponent with the ball see the goal and
        score?

3.   As the ball moves, each player adjusts to become the
        pressing player (if it goes to their immediate opponent) or

a support player who judges position from how close they are to the ball. The closer to the ball the more they mark the player, the further from the ball the more they mark space.

4.   As above (5) is closest, (3) and (4) are next closest and (2) is the furthest away but still close enough to close down as the ball travels. Introduce offside to make it more realistic.

ZONAL DEFENDING IN A 6 v 6

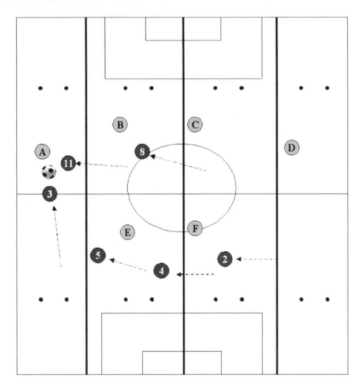

Diagram 31

1.   Introduce two more players onto each unit of players; each team can represent a back four plus two midfielders. Again look to maintain a team zonal marking shape. (11) can double up. As (E) and (F) move across the back four

they are passed on as they enter a new zone if there is someone to pass on to.

2.   The rope theory can be applied again here where they move in unison (2 midfield players also).

3.   Develop – Introduce two wide players to each team so it is now a four and four. The attacking team tries to move players around, the defending team tries to hold their zonal shape but also win back the ball.

ZONAL DEFENDING IN AN 8 v 8

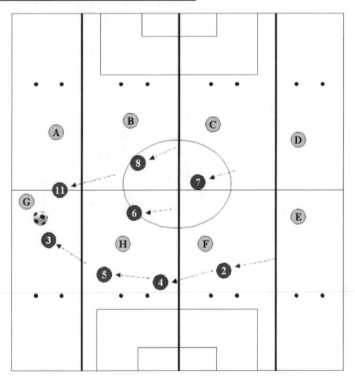

Diagram 32

1.   Using a diamond midfield. Each player knows where his responsibility lies in terms of zonal defending. They mark players who enter their zone. Mark in advance of the ball. For example, (2) is marking in advance of (E).

2.   If the ball is passed to (G) from (E), (2) can try to intercept the pass or at least stop (E) from advancing by closing down as the ball travels. (2) is still in a good position to defend between the ball, the opponent and the goal (inside the guiding triangle).Likewise (4) off (F) and (5) off (H). Eventually work a 4 v 8.

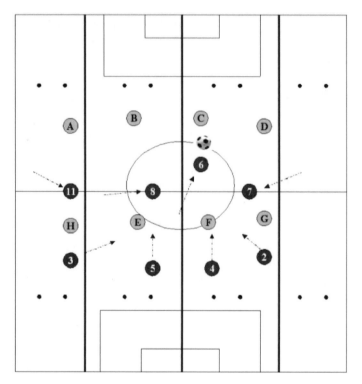

Diagram 33

1.   Using defensive and midfield straight fours to show an alternative style to the diamond midfield. We are still trying to maintain a shape by marking zones (spaces) while being aware of the immediate opponent's position.

2.   (6) closes down the immediate opponent on the ball, (11), (8) and (7) close up around the ball but are still aware of their immediate opponent's position.

ZONING BOUNDARIES IN AN 11 v 11

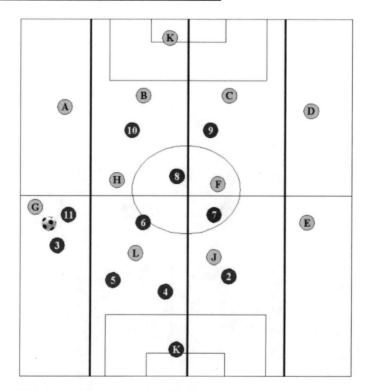

Diagram 34

1. Now we have the full 11 v 11 games with the players in defensive positions based on the position of the ball. Using a 4-3-1-2 formation with a diamond midfield.

2. Here the two defenders (3) and (11) work together to double up on (G). The rest of the players take their positions based on the ball, their immediate opponent and the goal. Notice (2) is tucked across the field filling the space in a central zone, not wide in the outside zone marking his immediate opponent (E).

GETTING IT WRONG

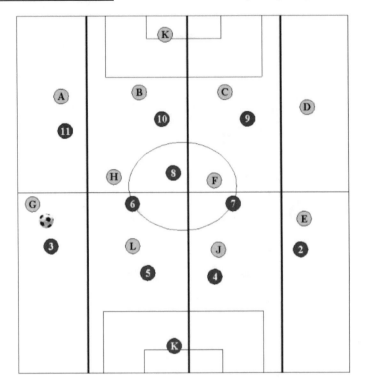

Diagram 35

1.   This is the shape of things when the defending team
      purely marks players and not space. Look how spread out
      the back four players are defensively, leaving big spaces
      free between them for the opposition to exploit.

2.   (11) is marking (A) so can't help (3). (5) and (4) are in
      their zones marking the wrong side of the attackers and
      (2) is in the wide zone marking (E) and out of position.

3.   The danger lies centrally if the ball is played there and the
      defending team's back four are too spread out and have
      no cover on. Diagram 33 shows a good position for the
      defending team to be in with cover on centrally.

CHAPTER FOUR

TRAVELING WITH THE MOVEMENT OF THE BALL BUILDING TO AN 11 v 11

DEVELOPING PLAY WITH A DEFENDING BACK FOUR

Diagram 36

1. This session is designed to show how to work on team shape building up from a back four only. Side cones are 20 to 25 yards apart as are the defenders and the coach. The coach moves with the ball and the defenders mirror the movement, maintaining the distances between them.

2. You can use the signal words UP, OUT, HOLD, DROP, and SLIDE (discussed later in Chapters six and seven), to determine the movement. Eventually we need to work up

to an 11 v 11 situation showing how to work a team as individuals, as units and ultimately a team.

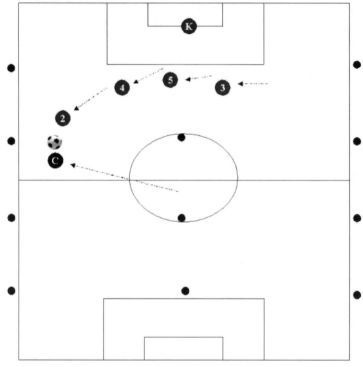

Diagram 37

1. Here the coach moves to the outside and the back four adjust their positions across the field (slide) to compensate for this movement. (2) is the player to apply immediate pressure on the ball.

2. Re-emphasize the idea that the players are tied as links in a chain and so have to move together.

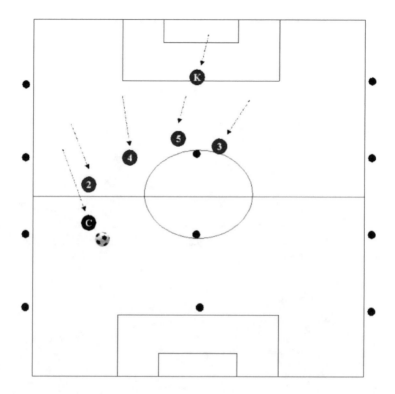

Diagram 38

1. The coach moves back up the field so the back four unit moves up also based on the position of the ball.

2. (2) is still the pressing player so must stay close to the ball should the coach turn.

3. The back four works up to the half way line based on the position of the ball.

INTRODUCING OPPONENTS TO SHADOW DEFEND AGAINST

Diagram 39

1.   Players with the ball pass it across in front of the defenders. Defenders adjust their positions to mirror this movement. This is working on marking zones and marking players and distinguishing between the two depending on where the ball is.

2.   Pass across to the next player and hold the ball there. Check the defenders' positions, then move the ball again.

3.   Use the side cones as guides for distancing between units as they are introduced.

Diagram 40

1. The ball has been passed inside and the defenders adjust, closing down the player on the ball and closing down the spaces around the ball.

2. This is continued using all the players, sometimes missing a player out with a pass so it goes across two players to test the defenders and how they adjust.

3. Once they have grasped this concept, you can move the players to the next progression.

4. In the next phase of the session have extra balls ready in the center circle to keep the flow of the session going.

INTRODUCING STATIC WIDE PLAYERS FOR THE DEFENDERS TO TAKE THEIR SHAPE OFF AS THE BALL TRAVELS

INTRODUCE TARGETS (T) FOR THE DEFENDERS TO PASS TO IF THEY WIN THE BALL. THE COACH CAN THEN START THE SESSION AGAIN.

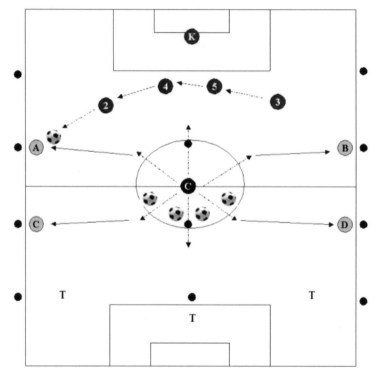

Diagram 41

1. The coach now has players to pass the ball to (opponents).These players initially must be in static positions to check the set up. You can use a rope to tie the four defenders together to get the idea of moving as a unit. Players maintain an open stance so they can see opponents as well as the ball.

2. When the ball is at (C) or (D), the back four take positions with regard to (A) and (B) and do not get drawn to the ball.

3. Defending team (numbers) can win back the ball only with
    interceptions of passes, not with tackles, to allow us to
    look at the shape they achieve.

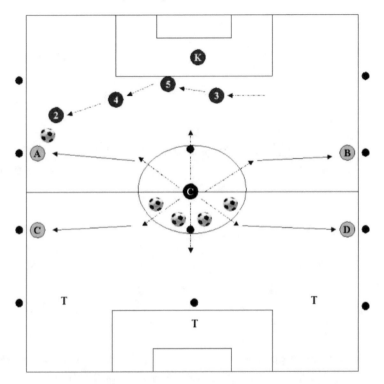

Diagram 42

1. Here we see how the back four should look once the ball
    has been passed wide and defender (2) has closed the
    ball down.

2. Notice the back four is NOT flat but angled with the
    central defender (5) the deepest player. This player can
    effectively be called the sweeper. When the ball is at (B)
    on the other side, (4) becomes the sweeper.

3. The second center back is the deepest player and the two
    center backs share this responsibility, depending on which
    side of the field the ball is positioned.

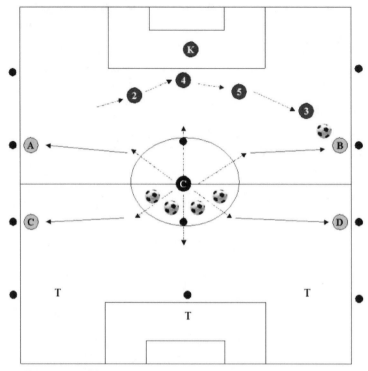

Diagram 43

1.   Here the ball has gone to the other side of the field and the back four adjust accordingly across the field.

2.   The sweeper is now (4) and the players are marking players and zones. The closer to the ball the more they mark the player, the further from the ball the more they mark space.

3.   Introduce two strikers on the attacking team to check the positions of the defenders who are now faced with more choices.

Diagram 44

1. The strikers now have more passing options and the defending players have more decisions to make. Again you could stop / freeze the play at any point and check the defenders' positioning.

2. Defenders position themselves based on the position of the ball, their immediate opponent and the goal. At the same time they must maintain their shape to ensure there are no holes created between them for the opposition to exploit.

3. Notice they stay tight as a unit around the position of the ball.

DEVELOPING DEFENSIVE PLAY INTRODUCING A MIDFIELD FOUR IN FRONT OF THE DEFENSIVE FOUR

Diagram 45

1.   Here we have the midfield set up as a diamond.

2.   The midfield adjusts as the ball is passed to (D). (11) closes, (8) drops in to support, (6) and (7) squeeze across. The back four push up and across to maintain the distance between themselves and the midfield. (8) could **double up** on (D) with (11) as an option.

3.   (D) passes the ball to the coach again and the ball is switched to another player and the defenders adjust again as a team to compensate. Wide players are still static, just receiving and passing. Defenders can still only inter-cept passes as we are working with the positioning of the defending team. If they win it with an interception they pass it to the coach or a target and we start again.

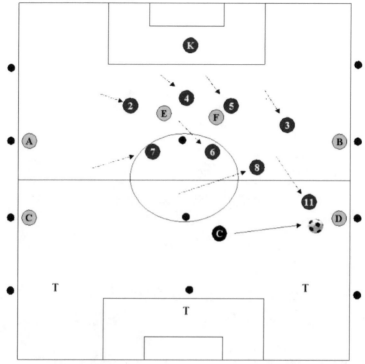

Diagram 46

1.   This diagram shows the positions of the players after they have adjusted to the pass to (D), with (11) being the pressing player showing (D) inside to the defensive support.

2.   By the time the ball is transferred across the field to (C), the defending team can travel as the ball travels and has time to get across. The immediate danger areas are the spaces around the ball which need to be filled as above, leaving the opposite side of the field more open.

Diagram 47

Midfielders have five possible jobs to think about when defending depending on the individual situation:

1.   **Recover** back to get goal side of the ball.

2.   Be the **pressurizing** player to stop the player on the ball (win, delay or force one way).

3.   **Support** the pressurizing player with angle, distance and communication.

4.   **Cover** (mark / zone) their own opponent so as they receive the ball they can close them down.

5.   **Step** into the **passing lanes** to prevent forward passes from getting through midfield to strikers.

6.   Any combination of these 5 jobs will apply at any one time
         depending on the situation in the game.

Diagram 48

1.   Introducing the same shape midfield as the back four. You
         can vary the shape depending on how you set your own
         team up. Try to maintain the same distance (about 5 to 10
         yards) between the back four and the midfield four as
         they move up and down the field. Maintain the same
         distances between the players and the position of the ball
         up to the half way line.

2.   The midfield players in this set up use the same principles
         of adjustment as the back four players maintaining their
         shape and keeping tight around the position of the ball.

TACTICAL DESIGN AND KEY COACHING POINTS IN AN 8 v 8

Diagram 49

Tactical Design

1. Pressure.
2. Support.
3. Cover / Balance.
4. Recover.
5. Double Team.
6. Track.
7. Compactness.

1. Introduce two attacking midfielders and allow all the players to go free. Coach the faults as they happen in free play, correcting the positioning of the players.

2. When the defending team wins the ball (only through an interception initially) they must pass to the targets or they

can pass to the coach working the ball out where they can. The Coach can then start a new game.

TACTICAL DESIGN PLAN

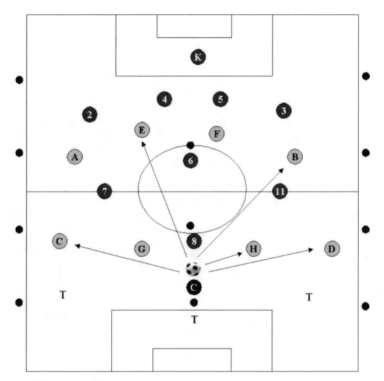

Diagram 50

1.   Once the players get used to the tactical plan, allow the defenders to now tackle the opponents and win the ball back as in a game situation.

2.   The coach can pass the ball to various attacking players in different positions on the field and the defending team must try to regain possession and get the ball to a target goal or the coach and the session begins again.

3.   This ensures the defending team has lots of repeated opportunity to practice defending because as soon as

they win the ball and get it to the target or the coach the attacking team gets the ball back and the process begins again.

DEFENDING WITH A BACK FOUR AND FOUR RECOVERING MIDFIELDERS AGAINST EIGHT ATTACKERS

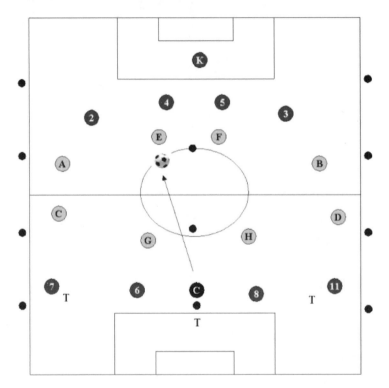

Diagram 51

1.   Make the defensive challenge more difficult by putting the midfield in recovering positions to help the back four. The back four can be patient when the ball is in midfield and keep their shape, delaying the opponents until the midfield recover back to help. Have a time limit before they can begin their recovery.

2.   Do the session with the four recovering midfielders first, then make it more difficult and use only two recovering

midfielders, then just have the back four against the 8 attacking players and see how many goals the attacking team can score in an 8 v 4 overload situation in their favor. Can a back four prevent eight players from scoring? If they score, work on what went wrong.

DEFENDING WITH A FOUR AGAINST EIGHT OVERLOAD SITUATION

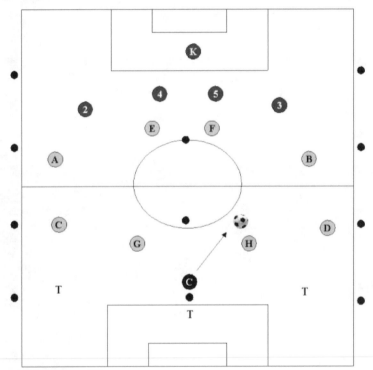

Diagram 52

1.   Now we are really testing the back four players and seeing if they have grasped how to defend as a unit and how to decide when to mark a player and when to mark space in a 4 v 8 overload against.

2.   Pay particular attention to the wide defenders being drawn to close down (C) or (D) and leave (A) and (B) free, thus breaking up the shape of the back four unit and offering opportunities to the attacking team to get behind

the defense in wide areas. Also observe the central players being drawn into midfield. Patience is the key here, let them play in midfield as there is no danger there in this situation.

TO CLOSE OR NOT TO CLOSE IN WIDE AREAS USING A 4 v 8 SET UP

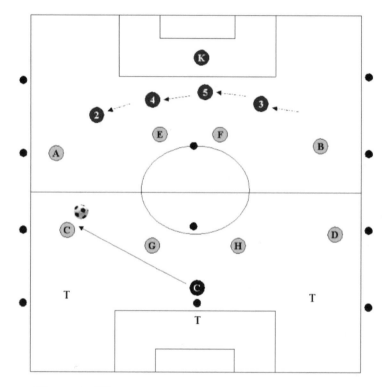

Diagram 53

1.   This is the best course of action where the back four stay intact and allow the midfielders of the attacking team to play and pass the ball in front of them.

2.   They only attempt to close players down as they get closer to the goal or the ball gets closer to their immediate opponents.

3.   Here (C) gets the ball but is no danger and (2) holds
      position, aware of where (C) is, but moves across the field
      slightly closer to (A) just in case (A) receives the ball. If
      the ball is passed to (A), (2) has to close (A) down. The
      rest of the back four move slightly across also, maintain-
      ing their distances.

Diagram 54

1.   This is an example of what can happen if the wide
      defender is drawn to the ball when it is at (C).Notice as
      (2) leaves the space and closes (C), the ball is passed
      into striker (E) who can lay off the ball wide into the open
      space that has been left by (2) for (A) to run into unop-
      posed. This now compromises (4)'s position who now has
      a 2 v 1 against. If (2) were to anticipate the pass early
      and be in a position to intercept, then it would be possible
      to close (C) down and have success.

2.   If the defending team is playing offside then (2) closes (C) down quickly and the other three defenders push up together and catch the strikers offside. But I would not advise this course of action as you are relying on too many variables: the officials getting it right and all the players timing the movement together.

3.   If you were to tie the four up this would prevent this situation from happening, so let the players feel how they should position with the restriction of being tied together.

TO CLOSE OR NOT TO CLOSE IN CENTRAL AREAS USING A 4 v 8 SET UP

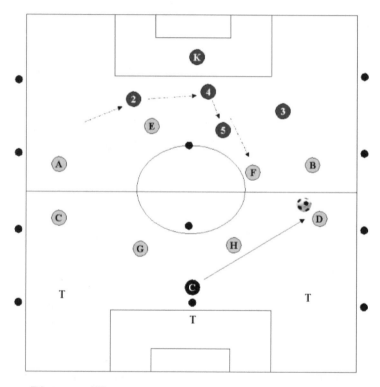

Diagram 55

1.   This is the best course of action when a central player's position is threatened by a movement short by the striker. (5) only goes so far then lets striker (F) go deep into mid-

field. In a game situation a midfielder could pick up (F) on entering their zone.

2.   As extra cover, as (5) goes short, (4) moves across to cover the space left by (5) and (2) moves across to cover the space left by (4)'s movement, leaving the outside space free. The best scenario is if (5) only goes so far then drops back to establish the chain link of the back four again, maybe even dropping into the position (4) left to fill the first space if this player has covered across.

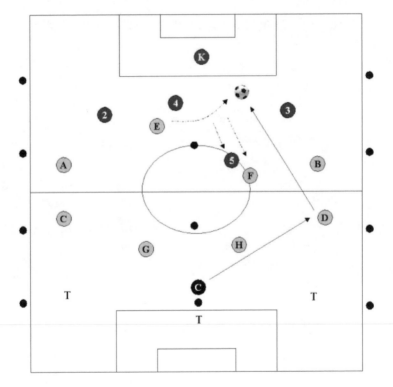

Diagram 56

1.   A position to avoid would be when the striker goes short to receive the ball to feet. The central defender must decide how far to follow but not allow a big hole to be made behind by being pulled away from the other three defenders.

2.   The above example shows the defender going too far and being drawn into midfield. The correct decision would be to only go so far as to not lose touch with the back four unit shape. If the striker keeps going short then he is moving away from the danger area and into an area where he will be less of a danger to the back four.

3.   (4) and (2) can still move across and fill the spaces left but (5) doesn't want to get too far away from them and become isolated.

4.   The idea of offside play applies here too.

TACTICAL DESIGN FOR AN 11 v 11 DISTRIBUTING THE BALL TO VARIOUS LOCATIONS ON THE FIELD TO DEFEND AGAINST

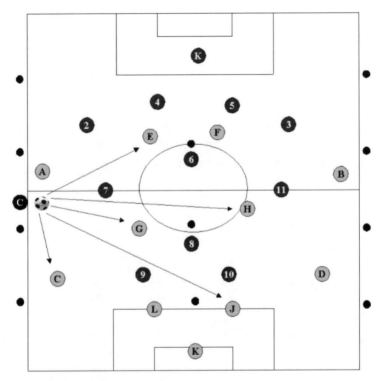

Diagram 57

1.   Here we have developed the practice into an 11 v 11 game situation, still working with the defending team (numbered team). The coach serves to the opponents in different locations on the field and the team tries to win the ball back individually and collectively.

2.   The target for the defending team when they win the ball could be to just chip the ball into the opponent's keeper and the defending team has to work to win the ball again starting from where the coach serves the ball.

3.   We have shown zonal defending as a team using a 4-3-1-2 system of play with a diamond shaped midfield, but the

same principles apply with other systems using the zonal method of defending and it is easy to practice this method with different shapes. Building up to the 11 v 11 set up we touched upon a flat four in midfield as well as the diamond four, both can be effective.

4.   You can set the session up in your preferred team system of play and / or set the other team up in the system of play you know your next opponents play to practice defending against them.

5.   There are numerous variations to use in this set up to achieve your defensive goals.

DEFENDING IN AN 11 v 11 USING A DIFFERENT SYSTEM OF PLAY

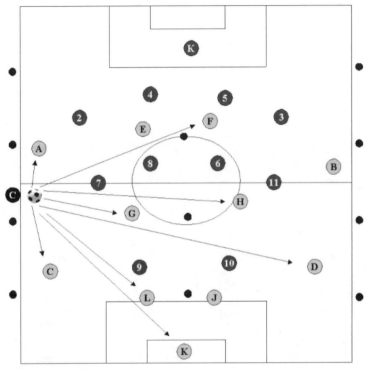

Diagram 58

1. Here we are using a 4 – 4 – 2 system to work the defending set up.

2. This is the same idea as the previous diagram. The coach can play the ball into various situations, always to the other team to attack and for the defending team to try to win back the ball.

3. Once you have used the target plan to allow lots of opportunity for defensive situations to practice, the defending team can now be allowed to attack the opposition as a reward for regaining possession and score a goal if possible.

4.   Eventually let the game go free and coach the defending team, correcting faults as they happen.

CHAPTER FIVE

DEFENDING THROUGH THE THIRDS IN AN 11 v 11

DEFENDING IN AN 11 v 11 SET UP

Diagram 59

1.   Our formation is going to be a 4-3-1-2. The opponents will be in a 3-1-4-2.

2.   Various formations can be used to suit your own style of play where the principles of defending in an 11 v 11 are the same.

HOW EACH UNIT DEFENDS EFFECTIVELY IN EACH THIRD OF THE FIELD
DEFENDING IN THE DEFENDING THIRD OF THE FIELD

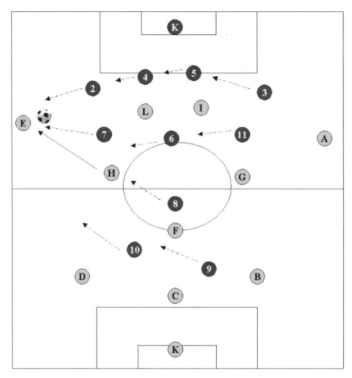

Diagram 60

1.   Pressurizing -Fullback (2) closes quickly as the ball travels. He shows the player inside or outside depending on where the support is and how fast and how good a defender he believes himself to be. (7) can double up to help.

2.   Making play predictable - For teammates to adjust their position. Close the spaces close to the ball. (8), (10) and (9) recover back. Leave the far players away from the ball.

3.   Support positions – Angle / Distance / Communication.

4.   Regaining the ball – Strikers and midfield must be ready
        to break quickly.

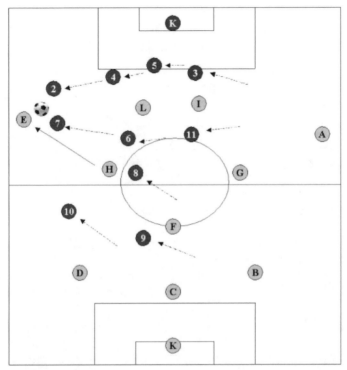

Diagram 61

1.   This is how the situation looks when the players have
        made their movements. Observe how the defending team
        has compacted as a team in terms of width and length on
        the field.

2.   They have filled the spaces close to the ball, reducing the
        room to play in. (3) and (11), who have moved across the
        field, remain focused on the fact that they are responsible
        for (A) and (G) respectively should the play switch to the
        other side of the field. Hence, their body stances are open
        so they can see both the ball and their immediate
        opponents.

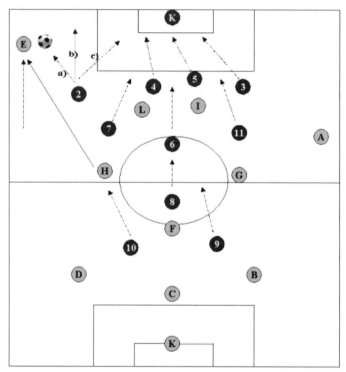

Diagram 62

1.   The opponents have penetrated behind our team in a
        wide area. (2) has three choices:
        a) Do I tackle?
        b) Do I stop the cross by getting in the line of it?
        c) Do I recover back to the goal?
        His decision depends on how close he is to the crosser. If
        too far away he should work back to goal because the
        danger isn't where the ball is coming from but where it is
        going.

2.   (4), (5) and (3) recover back to mark the danger zones in
        the box and will mark players who enter those zones
        (marking the near post, mid goal and the far post areas).
        (7), (6) and (11) recover to zones in and around the box
        for pull backs.

DEFENSIVE POSITIONS IN THE PENALTY BOX FROM A CROSSED BALL (RECOVERING BACK)

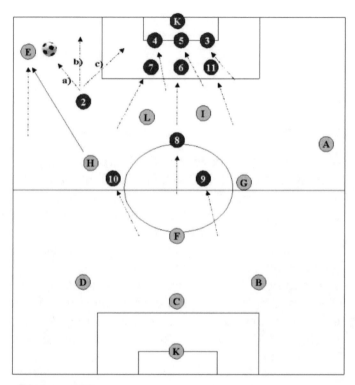

Diagram 63

1.   This is how it should look once the players have recovered back into position. I have only changed the positions of the defending team but obviously the attacking team will have moved forward and the strikers will be in the penalty box awaiting the cross.

2.   Now several major areas where the ball is likely to be crossed into have been filled by the defenders inside the penalty area and the defending team is in a strong position to defend their goal effectively.

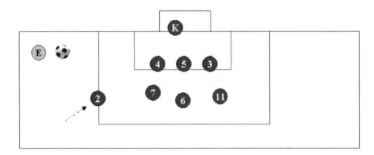

Diagram 64

1. (4), (5) and (3) mark zones. They attack the areas in front of them and don't drop back on top of their teammates. The same applies to (7) and (6). (3) and (11) also must cover the areas behind them if the ball is hit very long. They pick up players who enter their zones. (4) must resist the temptation to go towards (E) to try to stop the cross from so far away. The danger is in the box, not where the ball is coming from. By the time (4) gets close the cross has been made, perhaps to the gap where (4) came from, and the opposition has a free strike on goal. (5), (3) and (11) can fill in but we need to avoid too much adjustment.

2. If they win a header, the clearance should be high, wide and long. The defense should push up quickly to the edge of the box and beyond if possible (depends on distance and direction of the headed clearance).

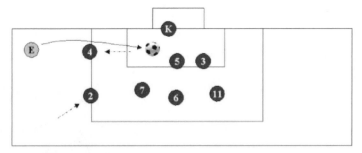

Diagram 65

3.   Here the defender (4) has gone to the ball and before he can get close enough to challenge, the ball has been crossed into the space he vacated. A striker may run into this open space now and score with a free header or shot.

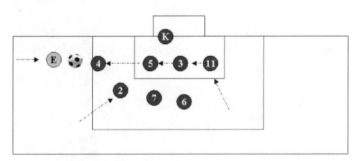

Diagram 66

4.   If the wide player decides to bring the ball towards goal, (4) is the closest and must close   the ball down. (5) and (3) move across to cover the nearest danger zones (rope theory) and (11) drops back in to take (3)'s place. (2) may have recovered into a good defensive position, particularly if (4) has held up the attacker to give time.

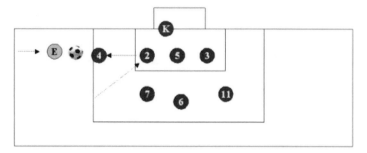

Diagram 67

5. If (2) can recover back quickly enough then the other players do not need to adjust their positions. (2) can do the same job as (4) did, guarding the area of the near post.

6. The only drawback would be that (2) is now facing the goal, so any interception attempted should a cross be made will be back towards the goal. (2) must be careful to clear the ball for a corner and not deflect it into the goal for an own goal.

7. If (4) can delay the cross by closing (E) down effectively then this will give (2) time to position correctly facing away from the goal. Now should the cross come in, (2) is in a better position to make a heading or foot clearance away from the goal.

DEFENDING IN THE MIDDLE THIRD OF THE FIELD

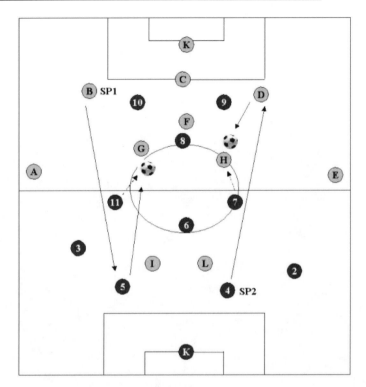

Diagram 68

1. The midfield players have two situations to deal with here defensively, facing the opponent and with the opponent turned away (when the opponent has the ball).

2. SP 1 – The opposition defender (B) plays a long ball. Our player (5) wins the header and the ball drops to midfielder (G). Our player (11) must apply pressure with the opponent facing forward with the ball. (11) must try to win the ball or at least stop the forward pass.

3. SP 2 – Our defender (4) plays a long ball to our striker but the opponent (D) wins the ball and it drops to midfielder (H). (7) must apply pressure and stop (H) from turning. (9) can double up from the other side with the help of (8) also.

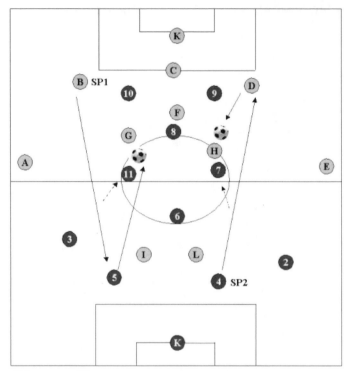

Diagram 69

1. Here we show the two situations where the pressing play ers (11) and (7) in their respective positions have closed down their immediate opponents on the ball.

2. (7) 's position is particularly strong as (H) is facing backwards and this allows the defending team's back four to move up the field and condense the spaces in front.

3. (11) 's position is less strong as the opponent is facing forward with the ball so the back players may decide not to move forward.(11) must try to win the ball or at least prevent the forward pass.

ROLES OF MIDFIELD PLAYERS IN THE MIDFIELD THIRD

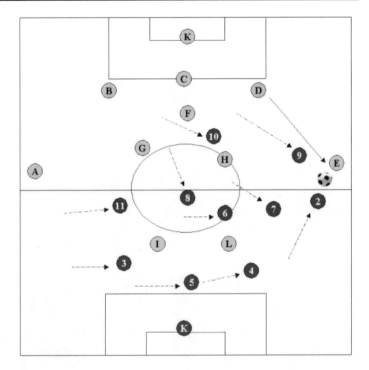

Diagram 70

1.   SP 1 - The ball is passed to the wingback (E) and (2) closes as the ball is traveling. The whole team adjusts their positions and takes their shape depending on where the pressing player shows the ball. In this case he shows inside and (9) can double team, (7) and (8) recover back and across, (6) and (11) close the spaces down closer to the ball and (4) marks (L) wrong (channel) side. Any ball played into the channel is cut off by (4). (5) and (3), using the rope theory, get pulled across to close the immediate spaces.

2.   (4) marking **goal side** would be inside of attacking player (L), allowing a ball to be played into the channel and (L) would be in the best position to win it. By moving channel side or wrong side (opposite the goal side), (4) would take away this outlet and using the rope theory (5) and (3) come across with (4) to close down the spaces.

3.   While defenders are told to mark goal side generally, in this instance the best decision is to do the opposite (I call it wrong or channel side). Here it gives the defender an advantage.

REGAINING POSSESSION IN THE MIDDLE THIRD

Diagram 71

1.   SP 1: The ball is played from (C) wide to (D) then into midfield to (H) and (7) closes down to try to win the ball.

2.   (9) can double team from the other side of the ball to help regain possession. (8) could triple team.

3.   SP 2 : (4) plays a long ball into the attacking third and (D) wins a header under pressure from (9) (our striker must at least challenge so the header isn't clean and doesn't travel far).Midfield players anticipate where the header will go so they can be there to pick up the second ball. It may

be in front of them so they can regain it immediately, in front of them but to an opponent so they pressure to stop the turn and try to win it back or it may be behind them so they have to recover into a position to try to win it back.

Diagram 72

1. The position of the players after the ball has been played to (H). (7) closes down and prevents (H) from turning, (9) can double team from the other side, (2) is closer to (E) should the next pass go there.

2. Notice that (H) can't pass forward. This allows the back players to move up and leave (I) and (L) offside.

3. Other players fill spaces around the ball.

4. (H) should be forced to pass the ball back as the worst case scenario, or (7) and (9) can win the ball back early with good pressure.

REGAINING POSSESSION IN THE ATTACKING THIRD

SP 1 - (8)'s pass is too heavy and it goes behind (D), (9) and (7) close down and show inside.

Diagram 73

1.   Pressure on the ball from the closest player, showing the
        player inside towards the support (first defender).

2.   Support – Next closest player: Angle / Distance /
        Communication (second defender).

3.   Cover – Next line of players closing down spaces close to
        the ball (third defender).

4.   Double Teaming– Closing the player on the ball down
        from two sides to regain possession.

5.   Recovery and Tracking Runs – how far to recover and
        track, when to pass players on.

6.   Compactness – Team Shape locking the opponents in so they have as little space as   possible to work in. The whole team adjusts off the way the pressing player shows the ball.

7.   Regain Possession – in the attacking third, close to goal to get an instant cross or shot in.

Diagram 74

1.   (D) may get turned or end up facing back. Either way, show inside.

2.   Pressurizing player (7) forces the player on the ball inside towards the support players not outside. Inside means if we gain possession it's a short route to get a cross or shot on goal. Show outside and if the defending team are under pressure the player on the ball can kick it out of play and give them time to reorganize, plus there is no chance of an immediate cross or shot if we win it back in a very wide area.

3.   (9) and (7) close down and show inside, (10) closes the keeper to prevent the back pass, (2) (11), (8) and (6) close spaces down close to the ball, (3), (5) and (4) push up but still leave distance from the opposing strikers in case the ball can be played in behind them. Organization – Work with pressing player, support player, then cover players, then defenders and keeper (individual, unit, and team).

Diagram 75

1.   Working variations of service. Different situations where regains are likely.

2.   SP 1: The keeper passes to a defender (as above). Work to both sides Strikers close down making predictable play. Try to show inside, but if that's not possible, then the team adjusts position off the ball in the wide area. The team quarters the field and squeezes play down that side. Strikers could look disinterested and walk away to encourage the keeper to pass the ball to (D) then close down as quickly as possible.

3.   SP 2: Defender or keeper passes into midfield. Our midfield stops them from turning and the strikers recover (they can double team from the other side).

Diagram 76

1.   (9) can't get across quickly enough to force (D) inside so has to force (D) outside. The rest of the team can adjust across also to condense the spaces down the side of the field to help win back the ball.

2.   Players furthest away from the ball are aware of their immediate opponents but mark spaces rather than players. For example, (11) moves across the field and leaves (A) alone because (9)'s position prevents (D) from being able to pass to (A).

3.   Players mark in advance of their opponents, filling in the spaces where the ball is likely to be played but not committing themselves too far so that they can be caught with a ball in behind them.

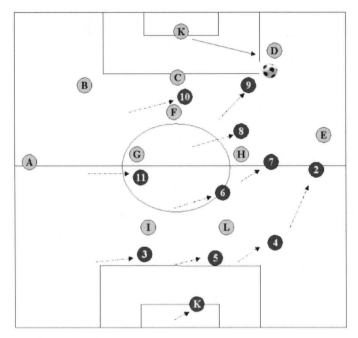

Diagram 77

1.   Positions after the movement. (D) is forced to play the ball down the line and here the defending team have filled all the spaces up with their movement across the field.

2.   If the ball is played to (E) then (2) is already in a good position to pressurize.

3.   If it is played behind (2) then (4) has moved across to fill that space.

4.   Any attempt to pass to (H) and (8) and (7) are in a good position to win the ball.

5.   Should (D) manage to come inside and play across the other side of the field, the whole team must adjust back across to fill the spaces on the other side.

CHAPTER SIX

SHADOW PLAY TEAM SHAPE AND MOVEMENT IN AN 11 v 11

Three units of players work together as a team, moving around the field maintaining a shape. The difference between defensive and attacking shape is just the spacing between players and between units. Defensive shape is short and tight, attacking shape is wide and long.

To help the players, initially keep the same spacing between players and units as they move around the field to get the concept across. As they get better you can move on to increasing the spacing, such as when we get possession of the ball.

All the movement can be without a ball to begin or the coach can move around the field with a ball and the team can take their shape from that.

USING VARIOUS SINGLE WORD COMMANDS TO MOVE THE WHOLE TEAM AROUND THE FIELD OF PLAY.

PLAYERS INSTANTLY KNOW WHAT TO DO COLLECTIVELY AS A TEAM ON EACH SIGNAL WORD.

BASIC SET UP OF THE TEAM

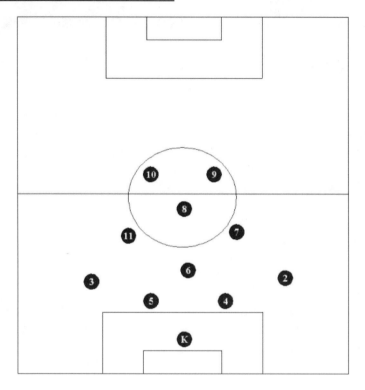

Diagram 78

1.   Set the players up in a shape you prefer and ask them to move around the field together, maintaining the same spacing. I have chosen the 4-3-1-2 formation but the principles apply to any formation for moving around the field as a team. On command (sit) they sit down where they are positioned.

2.   This gives you a chance to check they have kept their shape. Have words to move them again depending on where you want them to go. Words can be UP (up to 5 yards forward), OUT (a sprint, see if they can go at the same quick pace together, keeping the shape), HOLD (staying in position, holding the line of the unit), DROP (moving back towards their own goal), SLIDE (moving to the side or across the field).Between each word say SIT and check positions again.

UP
UP THE FIELD SLOWLY - CONSTANTLY REASSESSING THE POSITION

Game situation

Opponents have the ball and pass it back towards their own goal, for example. Or we pass the ball forward maintaining possession.

All the movement can be without a ball to begin or the coach can move around the field with a ball and the team can take their shape from that.

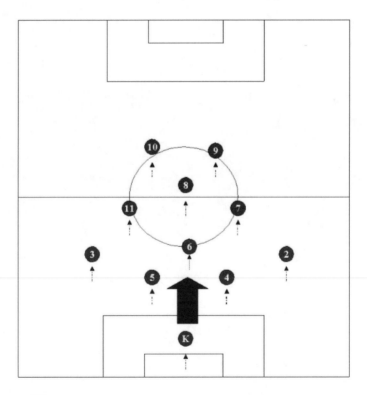

Diagram 79

1.   Here the players move up the field only up to five yards in distance, edging out, waiting to see if we win the ball. Then they can apply the OUT call. Also, it can be when

we pass it forward and move up as a team. Units move up together maintaining the same distance between each other.

2.   They move up a short distance then reassess the situation depending on where the ball is. If it goes back again (we force them to play it back as a team) we can move a short distance.

OUT
UP THE FIELD WITH PACE

Game situation

We have the ball and have played it forward into the attacking third and kept possession (or not, maybe just played it behind the opponent's defense). This can be a big movement forward. Another applicable situation is when the opponents have passed the ball back to the keeper over a big distance to allow us to make a lot of ground up with the out call.

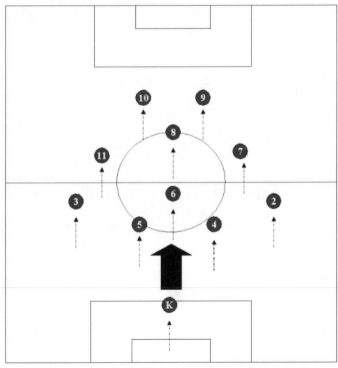

Diagram 80

1.   The team sprints out together on the OUT word until you say sit or stop. They then stop moving or sit down and you assess the spacing between players and between the three units. As they improve, speed up the commands until the players are moving around the field quickly and efficiently with correct spacing.

HOLD
HOLDING POSITION - PARTICULARLY AT THE BACK
DEFENSIVE LINE

Game situation

Holding the line at the back of the defense. The back defenders neither drop nor push up. This could be when the opponents have the ball but there is pressure on the ball so can't play it forward. Our team lets the opponent's strikers run offside.

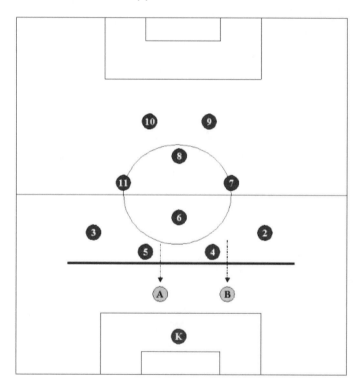

Diagram 81

1. The two opponents are included to show how this situation works; you wouldn't necessarily use them in this practice though it may help the players to understand it better. This is a difficult situation to identify for the players and relies on good officiating plus positive direction from the player in charge.

2.   This can occur even if the opponents have the ball and
       are facing forward with it but the defending pressing
       player or players prevent the forward pass. Decisions
       have to be instant here.

DROP
MOVING BACK TOWARDS YOUR OWN GOAL

Game situation

The opponents have the ball and are moving forward with it,
maybe in a wide area. There is no pressure on the ball to prevent
it from being passed forward.

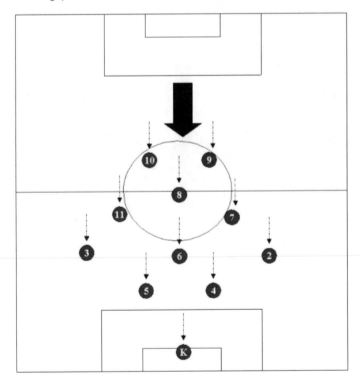

Diagram 82

1.   Here the team drops back together recovering back to the
       goal. Again there is more than one situation when this

happens. One example could be when the opponents have the ball and are moving forward and there is no pressure on the ball so the player on it can pass forward, maybe even in behind our back players. To avoid this we drop back as a team behind the ball. The closest player would go to the opponent on the ball, delaying the forward pass to allow others to get back behind the ball. For ease of practice, to highlight the movement here we work all the players together to get the point across.

SLIDE
MOVEMENT ACROSS THE FIELD

Game Situation

Here the opposition has played the ball into a very wide area and we all move across the field.
Slide can be used when the opponents are taking a goal kick so there are players around the area where the ball is to be kicked. The coach can move around the field with a ball and the team can take their shape from that also.

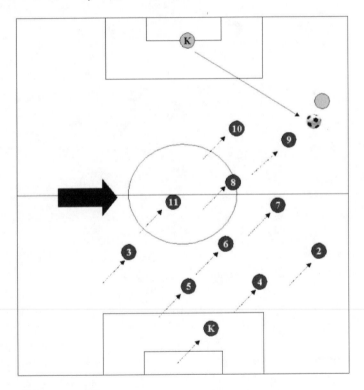

Diagram 83

1.   Moving across the field. In the game the ball may have been passed wide in the opponent's possession and we move across the field as a team to close down all the spaces around the ball to try to win it back.

TEAM SHAPE AND MOVEMENT INTRODUCING OPPONENTS AS REFERENCE POINTS

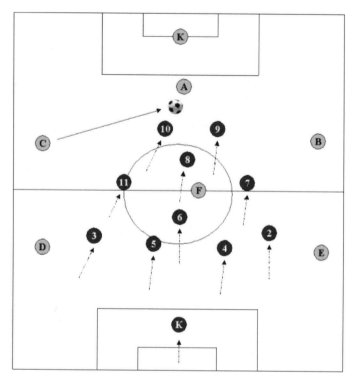

Diagram 84

1. Introduction of opponents to help get used to the calls based on what happens with the ball.

2. Here the ball has been passed back and the whole team move forward. The closest player (10) pressures the ball instantly, showing the player on the ball (A) into the support player (9). This is called creating compactness throughout the team.

3. How to create compactness from the back through the thirds of the team even when the opposition has the ball. The call UP would be used. If the ball were played all the way back to the keeper, the call to use could be OUT as the team has more time to push out further.

TACTICAL DESIGN TO PRACTICE ALL SINGLE WORD COMMANDS FOR TEAM SHAPE MOVEMENT

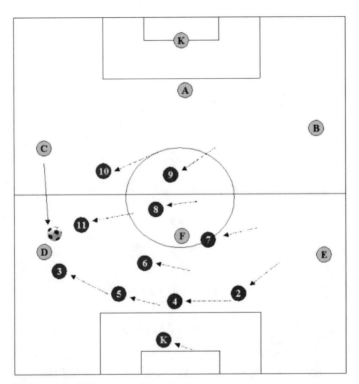

Diagram 85

1.   The ball is played forward into midfield and there is imme-
       diate pressure on the ball from (3) with the help of (11)
       possibly doubling up.

2.   The call SLIDE would be appropriate here. If the ball were
       played in behind (3), for instance, the DROP call would be
       the one to use.

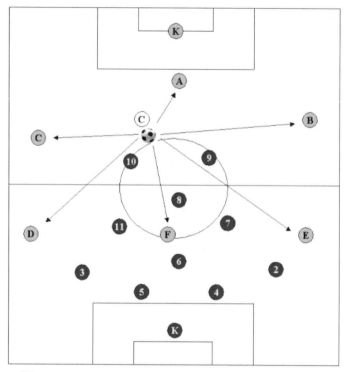

Diagram 86

1.   Ultimately, move the players around the field with the various commands, keeping them in motion. You can introduce other players to pass or run the ball around the field and the defenders must adjust depending on where the ball is. The team can only intercept passes, not make tackles as we want them to move around the field off the ball.

2.   Once they intercept it they can attack the goal and try to score as a reward. Introduce this method into an 11 v 11 game situation as the final progression.

CHAPTER SEVEN

TEAM SHAPE AND MOVEMENT IN AN
11 v 11 GAME SITUATION

EXERCISES TO SHOW HOW A TEAM CAN EFFECTIVELY MOVE AROUND THE FIELD AND MAINTAIN SHAPE IN A GAME SITUATION

UP/OUT/HOLD/DROP/ SLIDE - ONE WORD SIGNALS FOR TEAM SHAPE AND MOVEMENT

Diagram 87

1.   Just a one word signal can organize a back four defense so everyone knows what to do and reacts together as a unit. Midfield players react off the call too, as do the strikers.

2.   One word calls ensure everyone will know quickly and effectively what they should do as a unit and as a team.

3.   Hence the back players (and the keeper) can organize their movement as a unit (and therefore influence those in front of them) from five one word commands.

4.   The momentum is triggered from the back and runs forward through the team to the strikers.

5.   One player (usually a center back) is in charge of calling a signal word.

GAME SITUATIONS SHOWING WHEN TO PUSH UP, OUT, HOLD THE LINE, DROP BACK AND SLIDE AS A TEAM

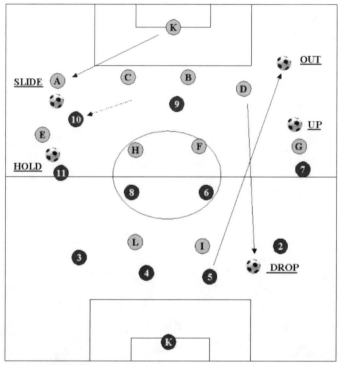

Diagram 88

1.   UP (squeeze maybe 5 yards), OUT (sprint), HOLD, DROP and SLIDE.
2.   UP – they have the ball and can't pass it forward.
3.   OUT –we clear it long into their half (especially attacking third) or play it forward and retain possession but continuing a quick forward momentum.
4.   HOLD – they can't pass it forward but they have the ball. Their strikers run offside.
5.   DROP - they have the ball and can pass it forward.
6.   SLIDE- they have the ball in a wide area and the team moves across the field.

"OUT" CALL USED TO MOVE THE TEAM UP THE FIELD QUICKLY

When to push up, hold the line or drop off depends on who has the ball and if there is pressure on the ball or not. One word signals keep it simple.

The center back is the best player to call it because he can see the full picture in front.

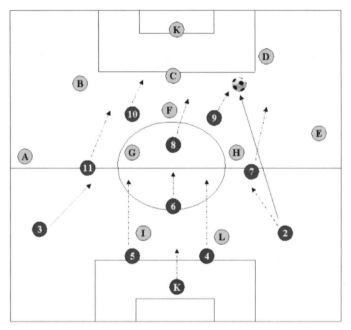

Diagram 89

FIVE SIGNALS

a) UP – Edging, maybe five yards at a time. For example, when the opponents have the ball but we are forcing them to pass it back (especially if the ball is a distance forward).

b) OUT – We have cleared it long and sprint out as quickly as possible, leaving opponents offside (whether we maintain possession or not, we still have time to get out).

c) <u>HOLD</u> – The opponents have possession but there is pressure on the ball and they can't play it forward. Here an opponent can run offside and we can let them go as the ball isn't coming.

d) <u>DROP</u> – No pressure on the ball and the opponent can play it forward, so the defenders drop off and track players' forward runs. You can be brave and step up to play offside, but we wouldn't recommend it! Also, if we need to create space to pass back if we have possession of the ball, the back unit drops off to receive in space.

e) <u>SLIDE</u> – The ball is in a wide position and the whole team adjusts across the field.

Positions of the players after the ball has been played long into our attacking third.

When to push up, hold the line or drop off depends on who has the ball and if there is pressure on the ball or not. One word signals keep it simple.

Diagram 90

1.   This shows the resulting positions after the movement forward up the field.

2.   Note also that even if the team loses possession from this long ball clearance, they have left the opposing strikers in offside positions.

3.   If they hadn't pushed up and stayed deep and the opponents won the clearance, the opponents would have maybe another 30 yards to play the ball into and their strikers would not be offside when they received the ball.

4.   This is a far worse situation to finish up in for the defend-
        ing team than the simple movement forward of the team
        as they clear the ball long.

EXAMPLES FOR THE SIGNALS "UP" AND "HOLD" FOR THE TEAM

"UP" AND / OR "HOLD" CALLS USE

Diagram 91

1.   In this situation the UP call is used. (H) can't play it for-
        ward, which allows the back players to edge up and con-
        dense the space and make the opposing strikers work
        back. Whether (H) passes back or not, while the ball can't
        be passed forward we can edge up.

2.   If the ball is passed back a distance, we can get up more
        quickly. But be aware, for instance, if it was passed to (D)
        who played it forward long first time we may get caught
        with a ball in behind our back line as we don't have time
        to readjust our movement.

3.   Even at (B), where the player is facing forward, if the pressure prevents a forward pass we can still edge up still.

4.   This is braver than <u>HOLD</u>. All the above applies for <u>HOLD</u> also. For instance, if a striker runs forward and the ball can't be passed forward as in the above examples, then let them run offside and hold the back line.

POSITIONS FOR "UP" AND "HOLD" AFTER THE MOVEMENT

"UP" AND "HOLD" CALLS USED

Diagram 92

1. This shows the positions of the players after forward movement, leaving opponents in offside positions.

2. Showing where the players end up highlights even more how easy it is to catch the opponents offside.

3. Both calls are appropriate, but "UP" is the better call to use because it also forces midfield players to push on and put more pressure on the ball and the opponents.

EXAMPLES FOR THE SIGNAL "DROP" FOR THE TEAM

"DROP" CALL USED"

Game Situation

Opponents have the ball, there is no pressure and they can pass it forward easily.

Diagram 93

1.   The above example shows there is no pressure and (D) can pass the ball forward early if need be. Strikers (L) and (I) can even time their runs back or across and forward (a), to stay on side as they have time to do so. Generally a defender will have to track the players' runs in this situation so the call <u>DROP</u> will be used.

2.   Note: the whole team should drop back to support the defensive back four so there is not a big gap between defense and midfield.

EXAMPLES FOR THE SIGNAL "DROP" FOR THE TEAM

"DROP" CALL USED

Positions of the players after initial movement with our defenders back in covering and marking positions.

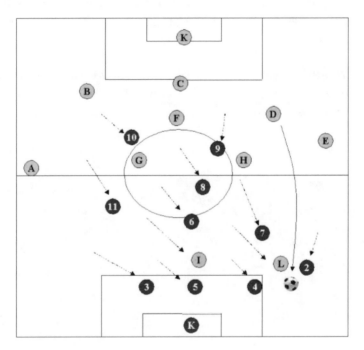

Diagram 94

1. This is how the movement back results in the back four dropping back behind the ball and in a good defensive position to counter the attacking strikers' runs.

2. The whole team should recover back to fill the spaces around and in front of the ball.

3. If the team is coordinated well and the call clear from the leader at the back then the back players can push up rather than drop off to catch the opponents offside. This can be done even with the opponent on the ball facing forward and free to play the ball forward, but in this case

can be risky and has to be timed well (and the officials have to see it!). I mention this because this is a possible alternative action to take in this situation and it should be covered. But it is not advisable as it takes only one player not to react to the call for the movement to fail.

4.   As (D) is setting up to play the ball forward and long, the whole back four can push up as a unit, catching (L) and (I) offside.

5.   You are relying on very good officiating to call the offside as it happens. Better to take the first course of action and be safer.

EXAMPLE FOR THE SIGNAL SLIDE FOR THE TEAM

"SLIDE" CALL USED

Game Situation

Here the opposition has the ball in a very wide area and we all move across the field.

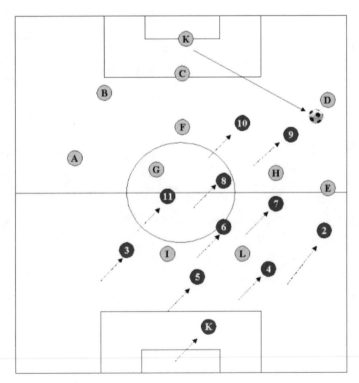

Diagram 95

1.   Moving across the field. The furthest players away from the ball are still aware of their immediate opponents but marking in advance of the ball (space) e.g. (11) slides across to fill the space but still has time to close down (A) as the ball travels across the field if the ball is passed to (A).

2.   In the game, the ball may have been passed wide in the opponent's possession and we move across the field as a team to close down all the spaces around the ball to try to win it back.

HOW IT SHOULDN'T BE

This is an example of a play that could happen in a game.

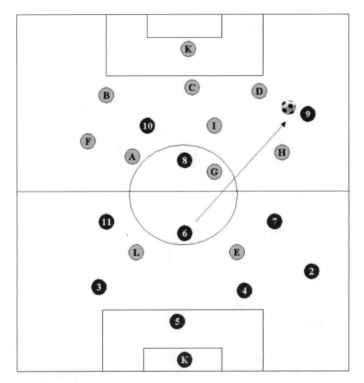

Diagram 96

1.   Players stay deep (our team is too spread out) so the other team has another 40 yards to play in if they win it. Our player on the ball is isolated so is likely to lose pos session as the opposition has superior numbers around the ball.

2.   The opponents win the ball and transfer it down the field into the spaces we let them enter because we are playing so deep. This means they get out of their own half easier and spend more time in our half and consequently get more chances to shoot on goal.

HOW IT SHOULD BE

Diagram 97

1.   The whole team moves together up the field. They are closer to the ball so if we lose it we have a better chance to win it back. Also, the opponent strikers are left offside.

2.   This forces the opponents to defend deeper so we keep them in their own half more often and consequently get into more scoring positions.

3.   It is important to maintain distances between the units up to the half way line so the whole team moves forward together. Spacing between players is so important to help them maintain possession of the ball.

CHAPTER EIGHT

DEFENSIVE DOUBLING UP IN AN 11 v 11

1 v 1 PRESSING WITH THE OPPONENT FACING THEIR OWN GOAL IN A WIDE AREA ON THE FIELD

High Pressure as a team.

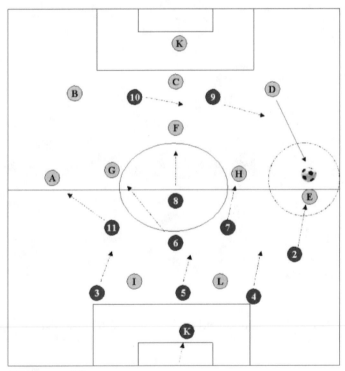

Diagram 98

1.   1 v 1 pressing with opponent facing his own goal. (D) passes to (E), (2) closes and stops (E) from turning. (2) must be a good defender to allow others to press 1 v 1 on their opposite number.

2.   Midfield gets tight to their players immediately. Defenders push up in front of the strikers, leaving them offside. (9)

closes (D) to prevent a pass back and (10) supports across. You can condense this into the specific area you are working in using fewer players e.g. doubling on central midfielder use midfield and strikers only.

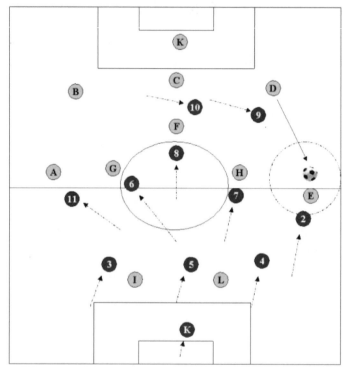

Diagram 99

1.   This is how the situation looks when the players have made their movements. All passing routes should have been cut down by the quick closing down of the individual players all over the field and the team as a whole.

2.   It is important that the pressing player is a good defender who can hold up and slow down the play of the player receiving the ball. Even better, if (2) actually wins the ball the defending team immediately becomes the attacking team as they are already in a good position to attack.

DOUBLE TEAMING AND PRESSING THE OPPONENT IN A WIDE AREA ON THE FIELD

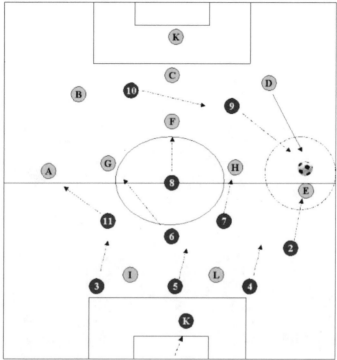

Diagram 100

1. The pass from (D) to (E) is forced down the outside by (9). (9) closes from one side and (2) closes from the other side.

2. (10) works across to fill the central area. Other players around the ball and beyond are marked.

3. Back players push up, leaving (I) and (L) offside because (E) can't pass the ball forward.

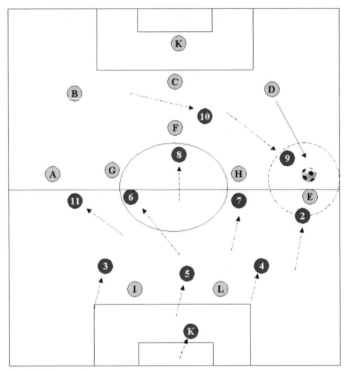

Diagram 101

1. This is how the situation looks when the players have made their movements.

2. This is a high pressure set up where players close people down all over the field individually and as a team all at the same time.

3. This is pressurizing all over the field with players marking their immediate opponents.

TRIPLE TEAMING AND PRESSING THE OPPONENT IN A WIDE AREA ON THE FIELD

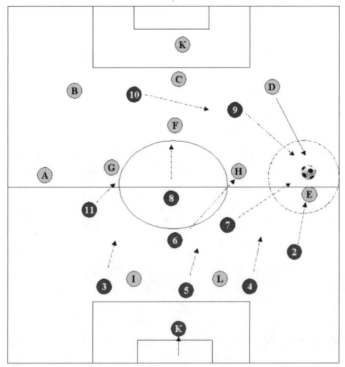

Diagram 102

1. (9) forces the pass down line. As the ball is passed, 3 players close from three directions, leaving their own players in some cases. Others adjust to mark for them and fill spaces close to the ball.

2. (9) stops the pass to (D), (7) to (H) and (2) to (L).
3. Movement must be well orchestrated so they close the player down together. Others must adjust at the same time to help.

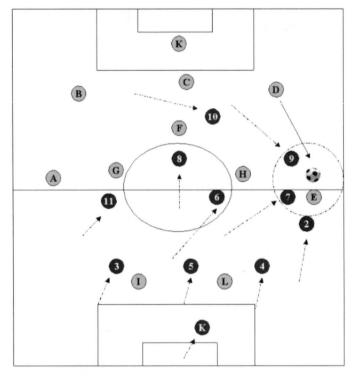

Diagram 103

1.　　This is how the situation looks when the players have made their movements.

2.　　We have three players attacking the ball from three different angles. Movement must be very quick and in unison as other players are left free to receive a pass when we employ this method.

CENTRAL MIDFIELD AND STRIKERS DOUBLE TEAMING AND TRIPLE TEAMING THE OPPONENT IN THE CENTER OF THE FIELD

Diagram 104

1.   Forces (E) to pass inside to (F). (8), (9) and (10) close together.

2.   Back four push out, leaving strikers offside.

3.   Doubling and / or tripling up on players should ensure your team has a much better chance of winning the ball back quickly. It is important that other players in the team adjust their positions to complement what has happened to safeguard positions beyond the ball.

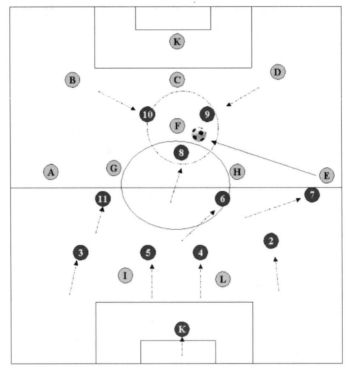

Diagram 105

1.   This is how the situation looks when the players have made their movements.

2.   The whole team has moved on in advance positions which will help them if they win the ball back quickly, particularly when the ball is close to their opponent's goal.

3.   By closing down as a team all over the field, they are already prepared in good offensive positions to attack the goal should they win the ball back.

DOUBLE TEAMING THE OPPONENT'S STRIKERS

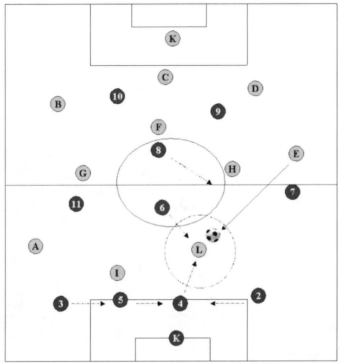

Diagram 106

1.   (E) passes the ball to (L) who comes short to receive. Defender (4) closes from behind, tracking the run and midfielder (6) closes from the other side to double up on (L).

2.   (8) close down (H) to prevent the option of the pass from (L). (7) covers the pass back to (E) and tracks any runs.

3.   Defenders (2), (3) and (5) close up together filling the central spaces.

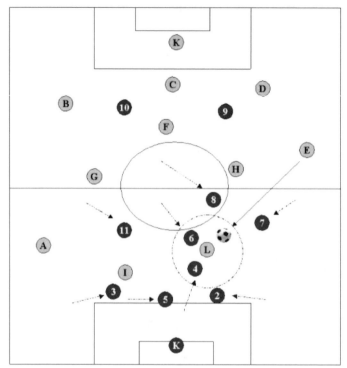

Diagram 107

1.   This is how the situation looks when the players have made their movements.

2.   They could even triple team the player on the ball with (7) or (8) closing the player down also.

3.
ly   Defenders at the back close the spaces down immediate-behind the ball, making their defensive position very strong.

4.   Double and triple teaming opponents is a very good way to win the ball back quickly and to put intense pressure on the opponent on the ball to force him to give the ball up with a rushed pass if the defenders do not win the ball immediately with a tackle.

5.   It has to happen quickly because, particularly in triple teaming, this means other players on the opposition may get free and be available to receive a pass in time and space. Players need a lot of practice to perfect this type of defending but it is an important tool to use in winning back the ball early.

CHAPTER NINE

DEFENDING AT SET PLAYS IN AN 11 v 11

This chapter is included to show you some basic ideas on defending at set plays. I have kept the format simple and easy to follow. From these initial ideas you can build and change the plans to suit the needs of your own players.

DEFENDING AT CORNERS USING ZONAL MARKING (1)

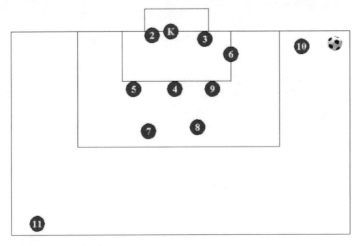

Diagram 108

1.   Everyone marks zones in the box so wherever the ball goes there is a player in the box to attack the ball. The above set – up doesn't have to mean certain numbers are in specific positions. For example, the actual player who wears (6) may be too small to take up the above position. I'm using numbers for convenience of explanation. Height and heading ability are determining factors. If you can tie in positions on the field relating to positions in the box, players will break out straight into their natural positions from a clearance from the opponent's corner (e.g. left and right side).

2.   (2) positions inside the post, (3) positions at arms length in front of the near post (if the ball goes beyond this position (3) can drop back onto the line to protect the goal).

3.   Position (6) is an important zone to protect as many deliveries arrive there, so have a tall player who is strong in the air here. (9), (4) and (5) take positions in line with the near post, middle of the goal and far post and attack anything in front of them (they shouldn't drop back and try to clear the ball if it goes over them, except (5) if this is the last player). (7) and (8) mark zones on either side of the penalty spot and can close down shots from the edge of the box from a secondary possession.

4.   (10) positions 10 yards away to block the view of the corner kick taker. This position changes depending on whether it's an out- swinger or in- swinger (get into the line of flight of the ball).

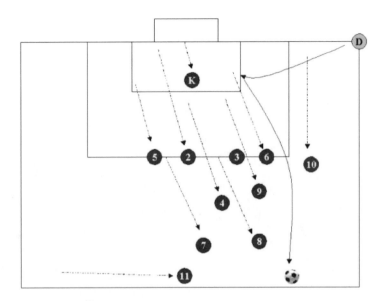

Diagram 109

1.   The opponents have crossed the ball and our defender
      (6) has headed the ball well clear of the penalty area. As
      the ball travels forward the team must travel forward with
      it. Closest defender closes the ball down as quickly as
      possible, in this case (8).

2.   Distances moving forward depend on how far the ball is
      cleared and who gets possession of the ball. The team
      must try to at least get to the edge of the penalty area to
      leave the opposing players offside in the box. Also, it
      allows the keeper to come out and claim anything played
      back into the box without having to try to catch the ball
      with players in the way.

3.   Notice the players move up and across to where the ball
      has gone, not up in a straight line. (5) has to be aware of
      any players staying wide and the opposing player on the
      ball playing a diagonal ball back across the field.

4.   The call can be "UP" if the ball doesn't go too far, or
      "OUT" if it is cleared a great distance.

DEFENDING AT CORNERS USING ZONAL MARKING (2)

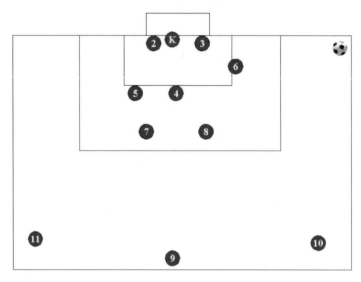

Diagram 110

1.   Leaving three up means the opposition will likely leave four back to mark them. This leaves seven players, of which one is the keeper and one is the corner kick taker. This leaves five, at least one of which needs to be around the edge of the box for any clearances to win the second ball.

2.   Therefore, we have four attacking players left to attack inside the box and seven defending players to defend inside the box (a 7 v 4 in the defenders' favor).

3.   Players (2) and (3) cover the posts, (6) is screening at the edge of the six yard box (many crosses will be cut out here), (4) and (5) mark important zones at the mid - goal and far post areas (or can man – mark), (7) and (8) cover zones around the penalty spot and (9), (10) and (11) are ready for a quick break counter attack or clearance. Defending players pick up players who come into the zones they are marking.

4.   If you are winning and it's near the end of a game the opposition will probably send all players up for their corner. They have nothing to lose! In this case you wouldn't stay with this set – up (unless you are very brave!!). Leaving any players up can depend on the position of the game.

COMBINED ZONAL AND MAN MARKING ARRANGEMENTS AT CORNERS

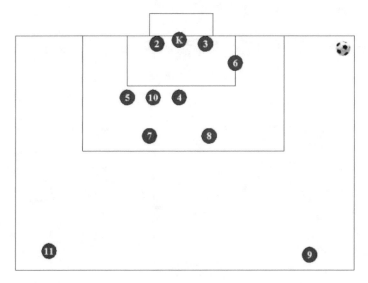

Diagram 111

1.   This is a mixture of marking players and marking zones.

2.   Players mark zones except for (5) and (10) and maybe (9) if three are needed to man mark in the box (pick up the best headers on the opposition). If you leave two up, spread them out so they are harder to mark if a quick break is created.

3.   If you need an extra player in the box to defend, take a player off the far post (near post player is more important) but only if the keeper is comfortable with this.

4.   Use big for big when marking players (if they can head the ball!!).

5.   This is the most popular way to defend a corner kick. Players (5), (10) and (4) can run and jump with the players they are marking because they move with them. If they were marking zones the opponent would have a running jump, while the defender would have to challenge from a standing position (unless they attack a ball delivered in front of them).

WALL ARRANGEMENTS AROUND THE PENALTY AREA

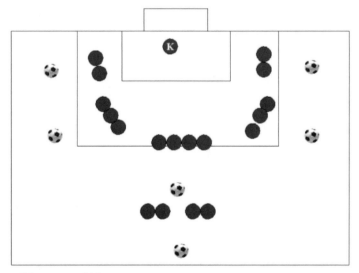

Diagram 112

1.   Where there are four in the wall you could use five also if required. Another way to set this wall up would be to split it in the middle so the keeper can see the ball in case an opposing player can bend it around the wall and the keeper needs to see it to help determine the trajectory of the shot, where it is coming from and when it's played.

2.   You can see above how the split wall would look (though it isn't in its proper position, it would be on the edge of the box).

3.   It is best if the keeper lines up the walls as their position
        most affects the keeper's position.

4.   You could have one player facing the keeper in the wall,
        pulling players into position on the keeper's command, but
        still being in the wall itself and be in position should a
        quick free kick be taken.

5.   For free kicks where the ball is central (and you would
        normally have a wall) and it could be a shot but it is a fair
        distance out, say 25 yards, a keeper may decide to have
        no wall up so he can see the ball and invite the shooter to
        try to beat him. In this instance the players should still
        take up positions as high up the field as possible to keep
        strikers away from the danger area in front of the goal.
        Dropping too deep into the penalty box brings the strikers
        closer to goal and closer to rebound opportunities.

DEFENDING AGAINST FREE KICKS CENTRALLY

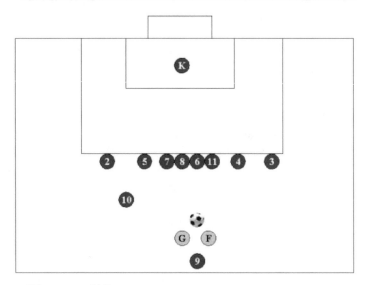

Diagram 113

1.   Usually it is the four midfield players who go in the wall with the tallest being on each end as that is where the ball is usually placed on a shot (trying to bend around or over the wall).

2.   The keeper can line the wall up or you can have an out-field player do it from behind the ball. Here (9) lines the wall up. Always do what the keeper is comfortable with.

3.   To get the position right, (6) should be lined up off one post, then (11) placed outside this line to make it difficult to bend the ball around the wall.

4.   (5) should line up off the other post and this player can charge the ball down if it's played to the side for a shot.

5.   Other players mark space or players. (10) can close down the pass to the side for the shot also.

6.   No one must drop back behind the line of defenders because this allows the opponents to get closer to the

goal and not be offside. So make sure the team holds the line high. Strikers cannot then encroach closer to goal looking for rebounds until the ball has been played, giving them less chance to get into dangerous areas should a rebound occur off the keeper or off a post or the crossbar.

DEFENDING AGAINST FREE KICKS
FROM A DEEP POSITION

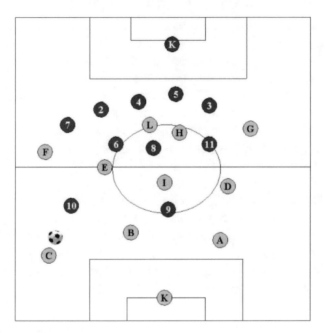

Diagram 114

1. Player (10) gets 10 yards away to disrupt the kicker and make the delivery more difficult. Players mark opponents and space depending on their position on the field. (8) screens in front, preventing passes into the strikers. (9) covers a switch in play across the field. (11) is aware of this too and ready to adjust quickly. The keeper is off the goal line ready to come and claim any deliveries into the penalty box.

2.   The back four push up and line up outside the penalty box defending high (how far up depends on how close to the goal the kick is being taken, in this case about 10 yards outside the box). This ensures the opposing strikers are kept well away from goal and therefore have a lot of ground to make up to get close to the goal as the ball is kicked without running offside.

4.   As the ball is about to be delivered, the back players drop off a few yards to allow space in front of them to attack the ball. If you play offside from a free kick then have a signal call for all the players to know what you are doing. As the player who is delivering the ball runs up to kick it, the back players move up at the same time and catch the opponents offside. This can be risky and players must work in unison, but if done properly can be successful. Using it once early in a game with success can cause the opponents to be cautious with every free kick.

5.   Defending high up the field offers a big free space in front of the keeper so he can come and catch a delivery with out having to run through players on both teams who may get in the way and act as a block. Too many teams drop into the box from this position and defend deep, making it very difficult for the keeper to come out and handle the ball. It also makes it easy for strikers to get close to goal.

DEFENDING AGAINST FREE KICKS FROM A WIDE POSITION

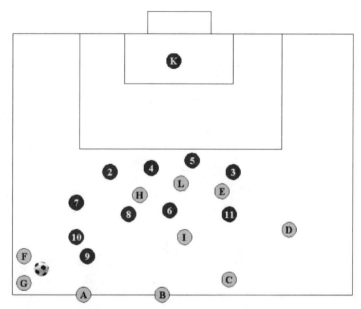

Diagram 115

1.   The ball is to be delivered from a wide area 35 yards from the goal line. Back defenders try to position outside the box to prevent strikers from getting too close to goal.

2.   A two player wall is set up and (7) guards the pass down the side (if you want more numbers around the box then (10) could do this).

3.   Everyone is behind the ball but (9). (10) and (11) must be alert if a quick break is on from an immediate regain of possession.

4.   Similar to defending from a deep free kick, the back four line up close together as a unit picking up players who enter their zone. It is important to get tight across the back line, leaving no gaps to be played through.

DEFENDING AGAINST THROW INS

Diagram 116

1.   Here (D) has a long throw and is aiming for the near post area to attacker (L). This player is screened in front by (3) and marked behind by (5).

2.   Defender (4) marks the space behind (5) but is close enough to striker (H). (H) may make a move forward off a flick on by (L) so (4) covers the space that (H) may run into. If the ball goes straight to (H) then (4) can close him down as the ball travels. Both defenders (4) and (5) need to move with the two strikers and not give them space to work in.

3.   (2) is marking the space at the far post but again at a good distance to close down (F) should the ball go there.

4.   (7) and (6) mark zones around the edge of the box, picking up the two players in their zone. (8) and (10) mark spaces but are ready to close down their immediate opponents if necessary.

5.   This is a mixture of marking players and zones.

WINNING POSSESSION IN THE ATTACKING THIRD FROM A SET PLAY

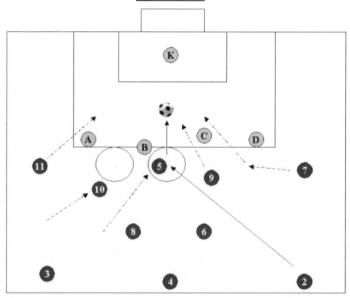

Diagram 117

1.   For a basic free kick from deep into or around the penalty box the above set up is ideal. Have your best headers of the ball (above (5) and (10)) running and attacking two (or three) areas, and have other players making runs forward off their anticipated headers as above (7), (9) and (11) (or also (10), if (5) is the pre - arranged target).

2.   Midfield players are in anticipation areas to pick up the second ball if defenders win the headers to keep the ball in the attacking third.

3. **Coaching Points**:

   a) **Quality Delivery,**
   b) **Team Arrangements** (pre – planned positions),
   c) **Attacking the Ball** (head across or at goal or put defenders under pressure so there are no free headers),
   d) **Stay Compact** (around the ball so wherever it goes we have a player)
   e) **Second Ball** (keep the ball in for a shot or cross).

DEFENDING AGAINST AN OPPONENT'S GOAL KICK

Diagram 118

1.   The entire team moves across the field to where the ball
      is likely to be kicked. Use the "SLIDE" call so everyone
      knows what to do with just a one word command.

2.   If they try to play out the other side and catch us, every
      one must adjust quickly back across the field. (7), (9) and
      (2) are the main players to react against this in the above
      set up.

3.   Strikers try to position in front of defenders in case the
      kick is a bad one (see the position of (10)). If nothing else
      this makes the defenders mark our players when they
      actually have possession of the ball.

4.   The back four take their positions up the field depending
      on how far the keeper can kick the ball. For younger
      teams all the players may be in the attacking half of the
      field except the keeper.

POSITIONING FROM OUR GOAL KICK TO
HELP KEEP POSSESSION

Diagram 119

1.   Our players know where the keeper is going to kick the ball so they get into position close to that area the ball is likely to land. This provides the best chance to gain possession, either with the first player to touch the ball or from second ball possession.

2.   Above, the keeper is trying to get the ball into the opponent's half towards the right of center and our team is positioned with several players around that area for first or second ball possession possibilities.

3.   We can see that we have a 4 v 2 advantage in the designated area with players in good positions outside that area to be able to have a good chance to pick up the second ball should the defender win it first with a header or if it bounces off his body.

4.   Vary the side the ball is kicked towards to try to confuse the opposition (keeper can have signals), and the players can move towards the designated area as late as possible to give the opponents as little time as possible to adjust their positions and be ready to counter.

5.   A little planning can help your team maintain possession more successfully from their goal kicks.

6.   Should (C) or (L) win the header, our team has several players in position to win back the second ball depending on where the clearance goes.

7.   If (9) wins the header and flicks the ball on then (10) should have anticipated this and be in position to win the second ball and attack the goal.

CONCLUSION AND DISCUSSION

To supplement what we have discussed here in this book on 11 v 11 defending principles you can refer back to individual defending from 1 v 1's through to 8 v 8's in the first book of the defending series. Both books take you through the full compliment of defending from basic 1 v 1 right through to the more complex defending as a team in an 11 v 11.

There are many different systems of play to use in the 11 v 11 game but I have mainly focused on one basic system; the 4-3-1-2 (with some reference to the 4-4-2 system also). To cover every system would be too much for one book but the basic principles of defending remain the same whatever system you use.

Phase Plays allow you to work with different units of the team within a session in different areas of the field. Defending with the defensive back four players and the midfield or a part of the midfield is an example of a phase play. Defending in the attacking third with the strikers with a back up from the midfield players is another example. Breaking it down to a smaller number of players is a simpler introduction than going straight into an 11 v 11. It is a natural progression to do the same session but with the full 11 v 11 set up. The addition of all the other players on the team completes the process and the session can then be practiced with all the players involved but with the focus still on certain units in combination. The phase play allows you to build to this stage and is easier for the players to grasp.

Zonal defending is a major part of the book, as is working with a defending back four as opposed to a three, but again the principles remain the same. My aim was to simplify the process by starting with a 2 v 1 and showing the principles of zonal defending and building up gradually through 4 v 4, 4 v 6 and so on until we arrive at the full 11 v 11 game set up. Again, doing it this way is easier for the players to understand.

The chapter on traveling with the ball (moving as the ball moves) was again an example of how to develop a plan from simple beginnings and take it through all the progressions to eventually arrive at the 11 v 11. We touched on different set ups in the midfield here and how they defend as a unit. The main idea from this is defenders traveling (moving) as the ball travels (moves) to take up good defensive positions, not waiting until the ball has been moved and then traveling when it is normally too late.

Carrying on the same theme of defending through the thirds, the theme was defending in the defending, middle and attacking thirds of the field. I wanted to show how it was done but within the 11 v 11 and within these certain areas of the field. Here there is a cross over between the units and how they defend collectively depending on which area of the field they are. In the defensive third it could be the defending unit and the midfield unit, in the attacking third it could be the midfield unit and the attacking unit (strikers), in the middle third it could be all the three units working together.

The shadow play chapter introduced the idea of moving the team around the field with one word commands to make it easy for all the players to be co-coordinated and know what each had to do in relation to the other. This movement could apply to any system or style.

I then took it into game situations to show various examples of how, where and when the concepts can be effective.

Doubling up in defending is a fairly new concept that is being universally used and shows how players can attack opponents on the ball from different directions and overload the immediate area of the ball with more players, giving the defending team more chance to win back possession of the ball. Emphasis here is on the players doing it quickly and collectively, because there will be other players open as a consequence of the movement.

Finally I introduced some simple ideas on defending at set plays which I believe is a very important part of the game. Many more goals are scored from set plays now because teams are better organized in the attacking phase.

As in my first book on defending I hope this book has helped you as a coach / player understand better the art of defending, an overlooked technique at times that deserves to be acknowledged as an important skill in soccer.

Regards and I wish you great times with the game,

WAYNE HARRISON.
E MAIL: wharrison@integraonline.com
WEBSITE: www.waynesworldofsoccer.com

Also Available from Reedswain